CONTENTS

Introduction	2
Authors	6
The 5 Marks of Mission	7
How to use this study guide	8
Study 1 - Legion (the Gerasene Demoniac)	12
Study 2 - An odd one....	24
Study 3 - Stevo	38
Study 4 - Who Touched Me?	52
Study 5 - Zacchaeus	64
Study 6 - My Brother	78
Study 7 - One More Time	94
About us	106
Additional ABM resources	107
Acknowledgements	108

www.abmission.org

Published by The Anglican Board of Mission – Australia ©2023
Book design by AZanker Design – azankerdesign@gmail.com

Cover painting: *The Land is in Me - loved, present, bunion and all*

THE IMAGINARY DOORWAY

INTRODUCTION

For many of us, the moment Lucy chose to walk further into the wardrobe and emerge in Narnia was the moment we received our invitation into a world of wonder and heroism and delight. C S Lewis's book[1] has aged, and some of the concepts are becoming more alien to us, even odd, but the imaginative journey remains untouched. The realm of Aslan is not safe, but it is inviting – and very real to those who walk through the imaginary door.

There is something about the imaginative worlds we inhabit when we read great stories that allows us to form values and determine how we wish to inhabit the real world. We develop empathy and we encounter situations that test our sense of ourselves.

Strangely, we can shy away from using the same imaginative and empathetic gifts when encountering the Bible. And yet, the Bible itself invites us to step into strange lands and understandings. There are some who argue that we must read it in as plain a fashion as possible, adding nothing and taking nothing away. Such a suggestion is as fanciful as the most speculative fiction, ignoring the reality that we are incapable of reading without shaping the story through our own experiences and imagination.

When scripture is read in church, no two people hear the same story. Each of us imagines scripture to life, through our lived experiences, through the people that we know, through the images we have received (in illustration, painting, film), and through the creativity of our own minds. In addition to this, within each of us the Spirit is working differently. Each of us hears and sees – and remembers - a different story.

This truth is reflected in the existence of four Gospels. Despite the similarities between the Synoptic Gospels, there remain four unique stories of the life of Jesus, each different, each from a distinct

---

1   Lewis, C. S. (1950). The lion, the witch and the wardrobe.

community. Each focussing particularly on things that a particular community of faith thought important to communicate to each other, and to future generations. So, when we talk about the 'Gospel' we are not simply talking about the written word. The 'Gospel' that lives within us – the Good News - is a living story, coalesceing in our hearts and minds through the unique combination of our imaginative powers, the work of the Spirit - and drawing on the four Gospel stories contained in our Bibles. The Gospels communicate to us the 'Gospel', the good news expressed by Jesus when he stood in the synagogue and read from the Prophet Isaiah (Luke 4.18-19) and expressed by Jesus in his life, death and resurrection, through which he redeemed the whole creation and invited us to fully participate in the love and family of God. In this way, God included us.

This multiplicity of received stories is not strange to us. In some ways it mirrors an Anglican approach to the Eucharist, as expressed by Richard Hooker's idea of Receptionism, in which the bread and wine become the Body and Blood when placed in the hands of the faithful receiver, but do not when faith is absent. The spiritual, sacramental, liturgical 'story' is mediated through the lens of the receiver of the story. The spiritual imagination is fired and enlivened by the Spirit, and each person receives differently.

"Let it therefore be sufficient for me presenting myself at the Lord's table to know what there I receive from him, without searching or inquiring of the manner how Christ performeth his promise..."
Richard Hooker, Laws of Ecclesiastical Polity V.67.12

In simpler – and less theological - terms, this is true of the way we read all the stories we love. Think of the work of Jane Austen, J.K.Rowling, or any of your favourite authors. Choose your favourite character. Before we saw the films and television adaptions of their work, we all had a different picture of these characters. Unique pictures formed in our own imagination. The surroundings, the clothing, the vehicles, the landscapes.....for each of us the picture was different. There will have been similarities, but no uniformity. And yet the essential, living story that emanates from the words on the page, often rings entirely true for each of us, despite those differences. This is where the work of the imagination collides with the intent and power of the author and the story.

This is why the Gospel is always both old and new in every age. Why it is both fixed and changing. Because each of us, as we hear the story of the Gospel, as we read the four Gospels, imagine for ourselves a picture of the new world, the kingdom of God, that Jesus initiated and which the Spirit guides towards the eventual future when we will see face to face and not through the dark glass of our fragile, beautiful, temporal existence.

These studies aim to take you on an imaginative journey into the lives of some of the people Jesus encountered. They were not people who ever wished to make it into the story of scripture. They were, on the whole, people who had real needs that were met through their encounter with Christ. Seeing them as 'real', rather than as props in a story that is only about Jesus, makes the encounters – and the people - matter.

This is also the story of mission; be it mission overseas or mission at home. If we engage in mission without regard to the real, individual, unique humanity of those we engage with, our efforts will be a denial of their God-given importance. If our mission is all about purpose rather than relationship, we miss the point. In the incarnate life of Jesus, God chose to walk the messy road of genuine relationship, engaging with the troubles and joys of those he knew and cared about. In this way he was most clearly able to express love and healing for those experiencing exclusion and isolation.

The 'Gospel' is the story of God inviting us in. Of us being seen and made welcome. Of our reception into God's own family. These are stories of people hearing good news, being released, experiencing recovery and stepping into freedom. These are stories from the Gospel of radical inclusion.

THE AUTHOR AND THE ARTIST

Steve Daughtry

is an Anglican priest and Education Missioner for ABM, for whom he has worked (in two stints) for over fifteen years. He previously worked as an actor and theatre director for 25 years and is the author of many plays, which have been performed in schools and theatres around Australia and overseas.

He is a published poet, and has worked as a journalist, editor & filmmaker. He has given the occasional sermon, here and there. For over thirty-five years he has been working with the Gospel stories, always trying to open doors that allow people to glimpse and get to know God. Many projects have been shared with Vanessa and he is thrilled to have been able to work on this book with her. They have been married since 1988 and have three fabulous children and one glorious grandchild! Not that they're biased at all!!

....

Vanessa Daughtry

is grateful that the lifegiver and pain bearer who loves us best, invited her into a beautiful, restored life at a lost moment in her twenties. Visual art was part of that healing journey.

Since finding the love of her life, they have created and launched three fabulous humans and a theatre company for young people. More recently her heart has been cracked open wider, loving the children's partners and one holy grandchild.

"I am grateful to Stephen for the invitation and loving support to draw and paint again for his stunning, reimagined stories of the subversive, invitational power of Jesus."

Much of the Artwork is retrospective. *'The land in my blood'* series draws on the theme of being changed by walking in nature and land holding a history of violence in Australia. The *'Icon of the presence'* series attempts to paint a theophany of the presence of God as a face of light in her mind's eye as she lived a difficult decision. The *'Loved one'* series is based on her childhood fascination with the moon 'following' the car, shedding its light on the water straight towards each of us – a metaphor for each being known and loved.

The few recent images build on themes above, introducing regeneration, supporting nature to heal nature. In the 'woman accused...' she imagines Jesus drawing a firm line in the sand against judgment and violence towards women by men (echoed currently). As he draws and we change, lifegiving water rises, growth springs up, regeneration of culture and country begins!

Vanessa now has the pleasure and privilege of accompanying others as a Clinical Counsellor. She has a B.A. in Visual Art and a M.A. in Counselling Practice. She is a registered Clinical Counsellor and Supervisor and a member of PACFA. www.heartgardener.com

THE 5 MARKS OF MISSION

- Witness to Christ's saving, forgiving and reconciling love for all people
- Build welcoming, transforming communities of faith
- Stand in solidarity with the poor and needy
- Challenge violence, injustice and oppression, and work for peace and reconciliation
- Protect, care for and renew life on our planet

(Anglican Board of Mission - Australia)

The Marks of Mission were originally articulated at the Anglican Consultative Council in 1984 with updates in 1990 and 2012. They are not a final and complete statement on mission but they offer a practical guide to the holistic nature of mission. ABM has translated the Anglican Communion's official Marks of Mission (below) to adapt to our specific context. You might like to have a go at translating the Marks of Mission for your own particular context.

The mission of the Church is the mission of Christ

1. To proclaim the Good News of the Kingdom
2. To teach, baptise and nurture new believers
3. To respond to human need by loving service
4. To transform unjust structures of society, to challenge violence of every kind and pursue peace and reconciliation
5. To strive to safeguard the integrity of creation, and sustain and renew the life of the earth

(Anglican Consultative Council)

HOW TO USE THIS STUDY GUIDE

Please bear in mind that this is only a suggested way to use the studies. Each person or group will have different allocations of time and talents, interest and engagement. Maybe this way will work for you or your group and maybe not. Perhaps you'll find that some things work really well for you or your group and others not so much. Perhaps you will find that you don't - or can't - use all the sections. In the end, use the studies in a way that enriches your understanding and engagement with Jesus and the story.

STEP 1. READING THE SCRIPTURE

Each study begins with scripture readings, which you are encouraged to read alone and/or together as a group. After the reading, take a few moments individually to record or remember your initial response to the text. We ground ourselves in the rhythms of the Bible.

STEP 2. READING THE STORY
Read the story together. If you have people who are confident to read, and read with good expression and volume, it might be good to ask them to read to the group. Otherwise, give people time to read the story and immerse themselves in the re-imagining of the scene. Or you might do both. If some people are resistant to storytelling, or find it emotionally charged, don't worry. Everyone responds differently. Some of the stories (studies 1 & 2) may contain emotional triggers for some readers. We have provided links to national resource providers in those studies. Leaders should ensure they are prepared for such trigger moments and are able to respond as sensitively as possible.

STEP 3. REFLECT
Spend some time thinking or talking together about the responses you have had to the story. Can you imagine it happening like that? Does it seem unlikely? See what it sparks in you and ask questions of each other about any ideas raised. It is important that everyone is free to speak if they wish and that their response is respected, regardless of any difference of opinion. You may choose to set time limits or ask people to sum up their responses in a minute or two. In this section – as with all the others – the leader needs to ensure that no single voice dominates the group or determines the 'right' way to respond. Good leadership requires courage but will allow for a much more open and honest conversation.

STEP 4. THE QUOTE
Take turns reading these. Does it help you to see things from another angle? If so, great! If not….move on.

STEP 5. AN ABM RESPONSE
ABM's work in the field of mission is connected with the same priorities that Jesus outlined when he stood to speak in the synagogue at Nazareth. As the national mission agency of the Anglican Church of Australia, ABM takes seriously the business of working for love, hope and justice in a world that remains unreconciled. These short sections give you an opportunity to see how ABM is responding and invite you to consider praying for or financially supporting that ongoing work.

STEP 6. DISCUSS

The 'discuss' section offers an invitation to go deeper into the story and think about how it relates to the world in which we live. The story of scripture has to have an impact in our lived reality – so this section is important. Again, you might ask someone to read this section to the group and then invite responses. Some good starting questions might be, "Do you agree with the writer?", or "Did anything stand out to you?". Or you might simply like to go on to the printed questions.

STEP 7. QUESTIONS

The questions are grouped in three categories: Individual, Community and Church. You can use them in whatever order you desire, and you can choose which questions resonate for - and work with - your group. Don't feel the need to answer everything and if there is no response to a question, move on to the next.

ADDITIONAL CREATIVE RESOURCES

Each study has a final section with a song and some poetry or prose. These might be useful for individual study or reflection times or to use as a way of 'stilling' your group at certain points. Again, they are offerings and in no way compulsory. Many people have loved these offerings in our previous studies, and we hope you enjoy them and learn more about the artists who produce them.

Remember... (for those doing the study during Lent)

LENT IS A TIME TO CONNECT

Since the fourth century, the six weeks prior to Easter have been set aside by Christians as a special time of prayer, fasting and reflection. As we spend time together during this Lenten period, we turn our hearts and minds to what Jesus did, not just in the week of His passion, but also in His life and His actions towards others. Lent is a time to CONNECT with Christ, each other and those around us.

LENT IS A TIME TO GROW
Above all Lent prepares us for the coming of Easter that we may truly GROW into the spirit of Easter; to GROW in our understanding and experience of the passion of Christ, the joy of the hope of new life and in our response to the Spirit's call to follow Christ in the world.

LENT IS A TIME TO SERVE
It gives us time to reflect on our needs, the needs of others and all that we have and do. There has come to be a custom of 'giving up for Lent'. Not only are we called to 'give up for Lent', we are also called to 'take up the Cross' and SERVE the world around us.

LENT IS A TIME TO GIVE
The mission of God is always one of giving. Lent reminds us that we are called to live out in the world the self-sacrificing, self-spending life of Christ. As the Easter Community we are free to practice a radical generosity as we GIVE ourselves, in Jesus' name, to each other.

BIBLE TRANSLATIONS
When doing Bible studies, people often worry about which version they should read. We have usually chosen to use the text from the NRSV in these studies...but...having a range of translations and versions will sometimes help you to discover more in the text. Whatever you regularly read will do the job if you invite the Spirit to read with you and don't get too precious about your version being the correct one. Let's always remember that we all read from translations - and no translation can be perfect.

LUKE 8:26-39

Then they arrived at the country of the Gerasenes, which is opposite Galilee. As he stepped out on land, a man of the city who had demons met him. For a long time, he had worn no clothes, and he did not live in a house but in the tombs. When he saw Jesus, he fell down before him and shouted at the top of his voice, 'What have you to do with me, Jesus, Son of the Most High God? I beg you, do not torment me'— for Jesus had commanded the unclean spirit to come out of the man. (For many times it had seized him; he was kept under guard and bound with chains and shackles, but he would break the bonds and be driven by the demon into the wilds.) Jesus then asked him, 'What is your name?' He said, 'Legion'; for many demons had entered him. They begged him not to order them to go back into the abyss.

Now there on the hillside a large herd of swine was feeding; and the demons begged Jesus to let them enter these. So, he gave them permission. Then the demons came out of the man and entered the swine, and the herd rushed down the steep bank into the lake and was drowned.

When the swineherds saw what had happened, they ran off and told it in the city and in the country. Then people came out to see what had happened, and when they came to Jesus, they found the man from whom the demons had gone sitting at the feet of Jesus, clothed and in his right mind. And they were afraid. Those who had seen it told them how the one who had been possessed by demons had been healed. Then all the people of the surrounding country of the Gerasenes asked Jesus to leave them; for they were seized with great fear. So, he got into the boat and returned. The man from whom the demons had gone begged that he might be with him; but Jesus sent him away, saying, 'Return to your home, and declare how much God has done for you.' So, he went away, proclaiming throughout the city how much Jesus had done for him.

Painting: Blood in the land. Land in my blood

I was whispering my names to myselves. Nurturing each darkness, caressing each echo. Stone edge bit my skin, a mark for every remembered one. Lines of blood on arms chains could not hold. I was laughing. I remember that. Laughing in the tombs, hoping another darkness might join my tribe. Welcome darklings. We were Legion. We were terribly strong. Terribly lonely. Terrible. We were Legion.

My fingernails sought out grubs and roots and rodents. I have good teeth. They have bitten to bone. I once tasted my brother's blood. I was driven away. After that they left food for me. Then they left me. Alone. But I have never been alone. Then, my choir of ravens. Now my one dove. A tree of raucous sorrow. A sky of burning, falling, healing love. What a difference a day makes.

We always liked to watch the sea for boats. Specks on bright water, trailing wakes of unnatural lines. Fishing boats. Cargo boats. Troop carriers. None of them made for our gravel beach. Too near the tombs. Too far from custom.

But this one did.

Weather-worn, with a stained sail. No pleasure craft. Too many occupants to be fishing, riding too high to be carrying cargo. Cutting a silver wedge in a grey sea, an arrow-head aimed at our deathly foxhole. We screamed a warning. A welcome. The song of one hundred voices of hatred. One thousand whispers of fear. The inchoate poetry of pain rang from the rock where we hid, and still the man, older than me but not old, walked up the slope towards us. The air began to hum as all my voices murmured the terror we felt. He was coming for us.

Others had come, easily repelled. Beaten off, scared away, disgusted by who we were. They came to bind us, and we leapt and writhed and shook them off like the fleas and ticks that sucked our blood. They came to bind. He was coming to unbind. We knew it, and we were confused.

He stopped, close enough for us to crush his skull with the rocks in our hands. To tear his throat out. Close enough that with one kick we could have broken his legs and kept him as a pet, to torment and mock. We considered it. Most of us were keen. He knew it. He did not step back. He looked at us, and we were terrified. Behind his eyes we saw the stars exploding and the light of every age both gone and to come. We saw pain we could not touch and we, masters and intimates of pain, saw it was too much for us to bear. We watched a rolling wave of love coming to engulf us and change us and separate us. We were terrified.

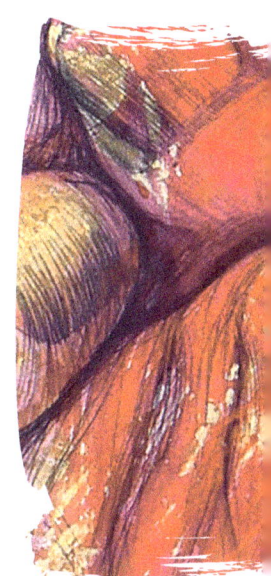

Our knees buckled. We knew who he was. "What have you to do with me, Son of the Most High God? I beg you, do not torment me."

"Me"?

"I"?

Already it had begun. We were being torn apart. We were being made whole. He asked my name, and I remembered it, but we screamed, in all our voices, "Legion". We were many, and all but one wished to depart from him. He held my gaze, and I was all alone for the first time in eternity. My others, begging for their lives, spied the pigs and all he said was, "Go".

A swarm of bees, rising like a desert wind, bitter and hot and angry, rose from me and rained poison on the animals, stinging and puncturing, driving them into madness and frenzy and a headlong rush into waters that welcomed them into unknown depths and the soothing balm of flooded lungs. All gone, but one. Silence.

At first, I did not recognise it. The still, small voice that was my own echoed in a calm void. My cuts began to burn. My tears began to fall. And still he held my eyes and I saw that my tears were his tears and that he knew me.

His friends, fearful and quiet, brought food and clothes. I washed. I ate. I spoke. Just me. He listened. They built a fire. They sang. All of them, the women and the men – I understood that they too had looked into his eyes and seen some of what I had seen. Or something that had been theirs to see. They called him, 'Jesus'. Or 'Master'. Or 'Rabbi'. Such ordinary names. I told him mine and he smiled.

When they came from the town, no-one would look at me. I know I have done things that have hurt them. Even my family would not approach. All they cared about were the pigs. So did I. The pigs had never shunned me. I was sorry. For the pigs. For the bees. I am sorry. All life has its place. I have my place.

I begged him to let me follow and he told me to find my home and tell my story. He said he had no home but that I could find one. A little of the light spilled from his eyes into mine and I was welcomed into a dance I am yet learning the steps of. I am not afraid.

The cities I visit are full of the broken and the rejected. I spend a lot of time talking with those who are visited by voices not their own. I am not Jesus, but sometimes a little light spills from me to them. On this side of the lake, I am building a motley family of those who have no-one. I whisper their names to myself. I remember them. I return to them.

I look up and the sky is full of burning, falling, healing love.

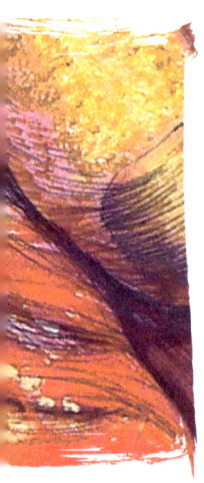

REFLECT:

What are your responses to the story? How different is it, to see the situation from the perspective of the demoniac? Are there things you have understood about the character, or the encounter, that were not in your thinking before? What is your emotional response? Are there things that make you angry? Or sad? Or happy? Or.....? Does this imaginative retelling ring true to you? Why? Why not?

> **QUOTE:**
>
> "The description of the Geresene demoniac was a description of someone who was completely isolated – who was out of control and alone and in pain. And if being out of control and alone and in pain was what the demon wanted, then I think it makes complete sense that the demon feared Jesus. Because in these healing texts, Jesus does not just cure people's diseases and cast our their demons and then say Mission Accomplished..., he's always after something more than that...because the healing is never fully accomplished until there is a restoration to community. People are healed of disease and he tells the folks just standing around watching to go get them something to eat. The widow's son is raised from the dead and he gives him back to his mother. And here the man healed of demons is told to stay with his people and speak of what God has done. In the Jesus business, community is always a part of healing."
>
> **Nadia Bolz-Weber**[1]

AN ABM RESPONSE:

Many of the communities ABM partners with have little or no access to mental health services or spiritual counselling by trained practitioners. In situations like this, one of the most profoundly important ways we can support our Partner communities is through education programmes. Women's Literacy programmes, Clergy Training programmes, Gender Equality programmes....all these empower communities to learn more about research and resources that meet genuine community need. If Christ's inclusive love is to be offered to all people, we need to help enable communities to understand how to deal lovingly with people and situations that can seem frightening and dangerous.

Let us keep in our prayers all those who are facing darkness in mind and spirit this very day.

---

1 www.patheos.com/blogs/nadiabolzweber/2013/06/demon-possession-and-why-i-named-my-depressionfrancis/ Nadia Bolz-Weber is an ordained Lutheran Pastor, founder of House for All Sinners & Saints in Denver, Co, the creator and host of The Confessional and the author of three NYT bestselling memoirs.

DISCUSS:

I encourage you and your group not to take the easy path of discussing whether this man was afflicted by demons or a mental health issue. We do not have an authoritative clinical text that yet fully understands the relationship between mental health and spiritual realities. Our opinions on this, intelligent and informed as they may be, will remain opinions.

What we do 'know', is that this man was considered dangerous and unwelcome by the community he came from. He was also a foreigner to Jesus. And yet, Jesus met him where he lived and engaged in both 'curing' him (removing the 'disease') and 'healing' him (restoring him to fullness of health and relationship). Jesus took a person both discarded and disgraceful, and re-established him within his community. Even more, Jesus sent him as an apostle to the Decapolis. 'Return to your home, and declare how much God has done for you.' In that one sentence is the release from ostracism and the command to declare the kingdom of God.

Newly healed and totally unformed and untrained, the man who was 'Legion' is sent to proclaim what God is doing. What is Jesus doing through this strange encounter?

In our own society, despite having one of the best mental health systems on the planet, many people hide their own struggles with spiritual and mental affliction from those around them. Shame, and the fear of being excluded and shunned, can become an insurmountable barrier to healthy integration and relationships. Many of us feel entirely inadequate even to discuss the realities of spiritual oppression or mental illness. We fear what we do not understand.

We are not Jesus, and we cannot, in most circumstances, immediately cure or heal. What we can do is to step boldly into territory we do not know, to listen, to do the appropriate research, and begin to understand what is happening for those who are struggling. We might have to work hard to gain a person's trust. We might have to learn appropriate language and behaviours. We might have to acknowledge our own struggles.

Many – if not all – of Jesus' healings are 'signs'. Signs of God's intention to heal and to restore and to include. Is it possible that the business of mission is not to build our numbers but to build friendships with those we do not yet know, understanding that there is a place at the table for everyone, and that we will probably learn at least as much about God from those we mission to as they will learn from us?

Painting: Bold Birds

QUESTIONS:

1. INDIVIDUAL

- How many within your group know someone close who has been affected by spiritual or mental anguish? Be careful to respect people's privacy by not naming these people without their express permission. What was your response to that person?

- What would help you to become more comfortable and ready to welcome neurodivergent and spiritually burdened people into your community?[2]

2. COMMUNITY

- What experience do you have of mental health services in your community?

- How well do you think our cities and towns manage the welfare of those who live with spiritual and mental health issues?[3]

3. CHURCH

- Does your church have resources available to help members understand and respond to both spiritual and mental anguish?

- Do you think it would be easy to disclose spiritual or mental anguish within your church community? Why? Why not?[4]

---

2 Brené Brown on Empathy https://youtu.be/1Evwgu369Jw
3 Mental Health resources: www.beyondblue.org.au, www.blackdoginstitute.org.au, https://professionals.blueknot.org.au, https://heti.edu.au/promo/free-unit-in-mental-health?gclid=Cj0KCQiA1NebBhDDARIsAANiDD2oEdk0CJ-AC5RUKCFde8QK_ZO99v5vbTxIGasgcvvakbgkyUZgKwIaAjwEEALw_wcB
4 Call or check the resources made available by your diocese or denomination

NOTES:

Painting: The Loved One

ADDITIONAL CREATIVE RESOURCES

Song: The Porter's Gate - Illuminate the Shadows

Google it or go to: https://youtu.be/WrvAjQvvvaA

Poetry or Prose: **Spirit and Marrow** by Regina Walton[5]

So thickly knotted,
The holy twins –
Real and ghost,
Untold apart.

Like the question:
Did the first body rise
From the earth or the sea?
And was it more or less than us?

Captured span
Without measure,
Volumes bound
And sealed in dust.

So thickly knotted,
Only the word splits through.

---

5   From, 'The Yearning Life' by Regina Walton, Paraclete press, 2016. Regina Walton is an Episcopal (Anglican) Priest and lives in Arlington, Massachusetts

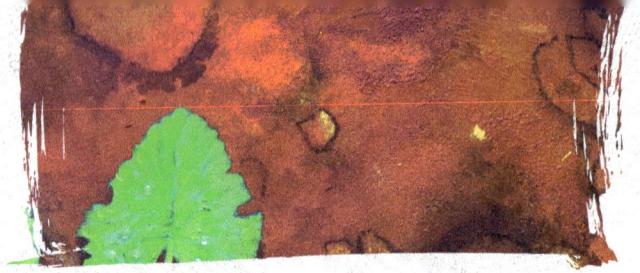

JOHN 8:2-11

Early in the morning he came again to the temple. All the people came to him and he sat down and began to teach them. The scribes and the Pharisees brought a woman who had been caught in adultery; and making her stand before all of them, they said to him, "Teacher, this woman was caught in the very act of committing adultery. Now in the law Moses commanded us to stone such women. Now what do you say?" They said this to test him, so that they might have some charge to bring against him. Jesus bent down and wrote with his finger on the ground. When they kept on questioning him, he straightened up and said to them, "Let anyone among you who is without sin be the first to throw a stone at her." And once again he bent down and wrote on the ground. When they heard it, they went away, one by one, beginning with the elders; and Jesus was left alone with the woman standing before him. Jesus straightened up and said to her, "Woman, where are they? Has no one condemned you?" She said, "No one, sir." And Jesus said, "Neither do I condemn you. Go your way, and from now on do not sin again."

Painting: Line in the Sand - no more violence against women

It's not that I'm ungrateful. I mean, I thought I was dead. Dragged through the streets like a dog, forced into the temple, surrounded by hypocrites, drooling for blood. It's a miracle I'm alive. Oh, I appreciate it. What he did. I just don't get it.

The day had started well enough. My useless husband was away. Again. Never marry a trader. Ten years married and if I've had him home for two of those I'd be amazed. Always somewhere, buying or selling something. It's not like he ever wanted to marry me. His mother's idea, I think. I was fourteen. He was thirty-five and his last wife had died the year before. He had no children. That's all I was for. Oh, and to clean and cook and manage everything while he travelled. And to give his mother someone to scream at while he was away. Never took me with him once. I wouldn't be surprised if he has a 'wife' in a few towns and he just doesn't want us to meet. I've heard of that happening. They're welcome to him, if he does. When he's home he 'does his duty'. The children are the only good thing I've ever had from him. He's about as enthusiastic about me and his 'duty' as he is about giving a refund on spoiled goods. You couldn't call it a love match, if such a thing exists.

So, that day we needed oil, and I was sent to buy some. I hate that shop. The owner always looks at me as if I've forgotten to get dressed. His eyes just follow me. Never looks me in the eye, you know what I mean? He knows when my husband is away. They're old friends. He's creepy, but I'd always thought I could manage him. On that day....he tells me he has some better oil that's, "Just come in", if I want to have a look. But it's in the storage room, would I like a taste? I knew if I didn't go, he'd tell my mother-in law I wasn't a wise wife, and I just couldn't cope with the thought of another barrage of put-downs.

I miss my mother. I miss my father. I miss a family where I matter. That's the past. You can't live there.

So, I go with him. When we get to the storage room, his son is there. He looks at me too, but not like the father. He smiles and his eyes dance. Sometimes he puts small treats in with my purchases. He's about my age and I can tell he likes me. You know, with men, how easy they can be to read. I like him too. I have wondered, imagined what it's like to be touched by someone who actually likes you.... but that's dreams, and you can't live in dreams.

His father yelled at him to leave. Told him to get water for the goats. The son said he already had but the father yelled again, and the son went. The well is ten minutes' walk.

He ushered me in and, when we stepped through the door, he shut it behind him. "Over here", he says, leading me to the darkest corner. "Oil does not like the light".

There is no oil. Just the bitter odour of his sweat, far too close to me. First, he offered me money. Said he knew how lonely I was. Started to touch me. I felt sick. Then I started to laugh. It was so ludicrous. This disgusting old man begging me. Laughing was a mistake. He hit me. He tore my clothes. As soon as he did that, I knew I couldn't scream for help. A half-dressed woman in another man's house. How could I explain that? And he knew it. I had almost decided to just let him get on with it – get it over with – when there was a knock on the storeroom door. His son's voice.

"Would you like me to escort Susannah home as I go for water, father?" Susannah. That's me. Time froze. Neither of us breathed. Then he stormed towards the door, threw it open and thanked his son for saving him from the 'temptress'. I tried to cover myself up. It made me look guilty. His son looked at me. He looked away.

"Guard the door while I call the leaders", the old man yelled. His son looked once more, then shut the door.

It was a blur after that. The elders, the Pharisees, the men of the village.... they all came to look. Look at the seductress. Look at the adulteress.

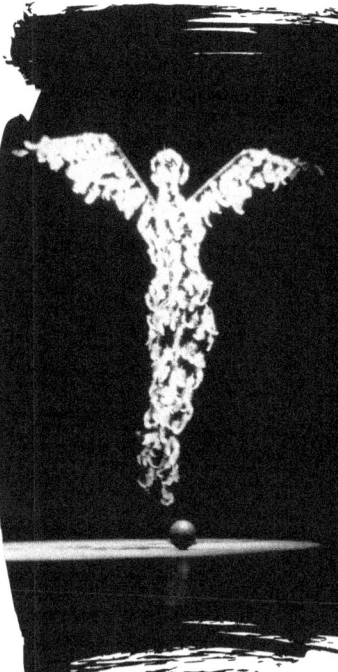

Painting: Pieces of Wholeness - winged feather figure chained to convict ball. Christ in us the hope of glory.

They dragged me into the light and refused to allow me to speak. Or to dress. The father and son were trusted witnesses of my "shame and evil". One a liar, one bewildered. I expected to be stoned on the spot. But then, a huddle formed, and the religious leaders held the others back.

The next thing I knew they had dragged me to the temple. That's where I first saw him. I had heard of him of course, but what had a crazy, young Rabbi got to do with me? I'd heard good and bad. He was mad. He was the Messiah.

They threw me, struggling to protect what little modesty I had left, to the dirt at his feet. I was terrified. Unable to speak. It was clear they were trying to embarrass him, make him slip up, say something they could accuse him for. "The law says to stone her, what do you say?"

What would he say? They all went quiet. He bent down close to me. I looked up, expecting to see condemnation. He was looking down. Writing in the dust. He wrote one word. Only I could see it.

They started to scream at him. Then I realised; I was just a prop. I meant nothing. My humiliation meant nothing. My life meant nothing. This had all been pre-planned. I had simply been the fly unlucky enough to walk into the web.

He stood. They waited. He looked at the man who had torn my clothes. He looked at the elders. He looked at the Pharisees. He said, "Let anyone among you who is without sin be the first to throw a stone at her."

He has the most beautiful voice. It bounced off the walls and there was no answer. No answer. And there was no stone.

He knelt again and wrote. Two words. Only I could see.

The shuffle of feet. Muttering. Angry words quickly hushed. Silence. A long, long silence. When he helped me up, they were all gone. Every one of them.

"Woman, where are they? Has no one condemned you?"

I said, "No one, sir."

Jesus, that is his name, said, "Neither do I condemn you. Go your way, and from now on do not sin again." He called two of the women who travel with him, asking them to see me back to my house. They found shawls to cover me. They were gentle. They listened. They believed me. They took me home.

My mother-in-law won't speak to me. My husband won't touch me. But I have found friends. Women who understand. Things are much better now.

Jesus saved me. I don't know why. He's an odd one. I remember the words he wrote. In the dirt and the dust, and on my heart.

His parting remark, "Go and sin no more". I can't make that promise, but I am working on it. I wanted to kill the old man, to spit in his face. But I remember what he wrote. I am trying.

Painting: Blood in the land. Land in my blood 2

REFLECT:

What are your responses to the story? What do you think Jesus wrote in the dust? Are there things you have understood about the character, or the encounter, that were not in your thinking before? What is your emotional response? Are there things that make you angry? Or sad? Or happy? Or.....? Does this imaginative retelling ring true to you? Why? Why not?

QUOTE:

"We make something sacramental when we make it like the kingdom. Marriage is sacramental when it is characterized by mutual love and submission. A meal is sacramental when the rich and poor, powerful and marginalized, sinners and saints share equal status around the table. A local church is sacramental when it is a place where the last are first and the first are last and where those who hunger and thirst are fed. And the church universal is sacramental when it knows no geographic boundaries, no political parties, no single language or culture, and when it advances not through power and might, but through acts of love, joy, and peace and missions of mercy, kindness, humility."

**Rachel Held Evans[1], Searching for Sunday:
Loving, Leaving, and Finding the Church**

---

1   Rachel Held Evans (1981-2019) was a New York Times best-selling author whose books include Faith Unraveled (2010), A Year of Biblical Womanhood (2012), Searching for Sunday (2015), Inspired (2018). She wrote about faith, doubt and life in the Bible Belt.

AN ABM RESPONSE:

While we in Australia celebrate that we are moving towards a more fully equitable social structure in which age, disability, race, sex, intersex status, gender identity and sexual orientation are no longer barriers to full inclusion, much of the world is grappling with their own cultural responses. ABM has been working with the Anglican Church in Zambia, as they have established highly effective gender equality training. Around the world, women continue to bear the brunt of violence and prejudice. Locally designed programmes, led by community volunteers, are opening doors to healthier community outcomes.

Let us keep in our prayers all those who are facing condemnation and unjust discrimination. Let us pray that the Gospel will continue to challenge and transform the world – and ourselves.

DISCUSS:

The story of the Woman caught in adultery is much beloved as an example of the compassion and wisdom of Jesus. Some love it even more because of Jesus's final remark, "do not sin again". Would the story lose any strength if he hadn't said that? I doubt it. The story is about the misuse of power and religion, the willingness to accuse and destroy, the desire to entrap. It parallels beautifully with Matthew 7:3-5, "Why do you see the speck in your neighbour's eye, but do not notice the log in your own eye? Or how can you say to your neighbour, 'Let me take the speck out of your eye', while the log is in your own eye? You hypocrite, first take the log out of your own eye, and then you will see clearly to take the speck out of your neighbour's eye."

Whether or not the woman was an adulteress does not seem to matter to Jesus very much. He does not ask if she is guilty. He asks if anyone is innocent. Not one can reply in the affirmative. The final words he speaks to her echo through the temple grounds and follow each and every person who was there. "Go your way, and from now on do not sin again." As does his statement of freedom, "Neither do I condemn you".

For many of us, our lives in the church have been dominated by calls for moral and sexual purity. Without doubt, these things are good goals – but have we been genuinely focussed on what moral and sexual purity truly mean, or have we been keen on rules and condemnation? It's probably a bit of both, if we're honest. History sadly shows that we have ignored or covered up some confronting and cruel behaviour (sexual abuse of children and domestic violence among others[2]) while causing immense pain and damage in the lives of some others who have been 'outside' societal or religious norms. Women, children and the Indigenous and LGBTQI+ communities are among many marginalised groups who have borne the brunt of abuses of religious and spiritual power.

It is true that we have taken important, wise and hopeful steps away from our past mistakes and that we are now trying to make the church a safe place for all[3]. We can still do better. The woman in our story walked away from Jesus both redeemed and encouraged to live well. We can only hope that anyone who encounters us, or our church communities, can leave feeling similarly.

In this story from the Gospel, the question is asked of all of us, "Who is without sin?" The answer is staggeringly straightforward. None of us are. At times, this understanding has been used to make us all feel guilty and regretful. Perhaps there is a better way to use this knowledge. If we understand that we all fall short of the hopes God has for us (and the hopes that, truthfully, we have for ourselves), we can transform that understanding into a willingness to stop judging the failings of others. Perhaps we can be encouraged to put down the 'stones' we might have held, ready to throw? Perhaps, we can encourage each other to walk more closely with Jesus, regardless of our weaknesses and failures? Perhaps, Jesus meant to build a world in which the condemnation of others no longer holds sway, and the opportunity to try again is always open?

---

2 https://www.1800respect.org.au - Call 1800 737 732 for the National Domestic, Family and Sexual Violence Counselling Service.
3 https://anglican.org.au/wp-content/uploads/2021/06/Ten-Commitments-April-2021.pdf

QUESTIONS:

1. INDIVIDUAL

- Most of us can reflect on a moment – or moments – of moral shame. Have you been able to take these experiences to Jesus? If so (without describing the original circumstances) what happened, or what was your experience of doing so?

- (For private reflection) Is there someone in your life whose behaviour you have unjustly condemned? Is there a way forward?

2. COMMUNITY

- Can you name individuals or groups within your community who regularly attract condemnation?

- What role does the church have to play in helping to ameliorate societal tendencies to blame and shame?

3. CHURCH

- Are you confident that everyone who walks through the doors of your church – or joins your Bible Study – feels safe and welcome? What gives you that confidence? What gives you reason to doubt?

- Are roles of service and leadership open to all in your church community? Are the loudest voices always the wisest? What could you do to ensure that your community becomes a safer, more inclusive space?

It will be important for the group leaders to be prepared to give access to local reporting lines (police and church) for criminal and abusive behaviours that group members may have been victims of. We cannot assume that 'our' group is ok. Have a copy of the Safer Ministry guidelines and procedures for your area at hand.[4]

---

[4] www.1800respect.org.au or call 1800 737 732 - domestic, family or sexual violence help line. Also: https://www.whiteribbon.org.au

NOTES:

Painting: Respected Woman with Trinity

ADDITIONAL CREATIVE RESOURCES

Song: Sanctuary - Carrie Newcomer

Google it or go to: https://youtu.be/HjOioWTVAl4

Carrie Newcomer is a songwriter, recording artist, performer and educator. She has been described as a "prairie mystic" by the Boston Globe and one who "asks all the right questions" by Rolling Stone Magazine

Poetry or Prose: **Unholy Sonnets 17** *by Mark Jarman*[5]

God like a kiss, God like a welcoming,
God like a hand guiding another hand
And raising it or making it descend,
God like the pulse point and its silent drumming,
And the tongue going to it, God like the humming
Of pleasure if the skin felt it as sound,
God like the hidden wanting to be found
And like the joy of being and becoming.
And God the understood, the understanding,
And God the pressure trying to relieve
What is not pain but names itself with weeping,
And God the rush of time and God time standing,
And God the touch body and soul believe,
And God the secret neither one is keeping.

---

5   From, 'A Century of Poetry: 100 Poems for Searching the Heart', (pg148), edited by Rowan Williams. SPCK Publishing 2022.

JESUS FORGIVES AND HEALS A PARALYSED MAN
LUKE 5:17-26

One day, while he was teaching, Pharisees and teachers of the law were sitting nearby (they had come from every village of Galilee and Judea and from Jerusalem); and the power of the Lord was with him to heal. Just then some men came, carrying a paralysed man on a bed. They were trying to bring him in and lay him before Jesus; but finding no way to bring him in because of the crowd, they went up on the roof and let him down with his bed through the tiles into the middle of the crowd in front of Jesus. When he saw their faith, he said, 'Friend, your sins are forgiven you.' Then the scribes and the Pharisees began to question, 'Who is this who is speaking blasphemies? Who can forgive sins but God alone?' When Jesus perceived their questionings, he answered them, 'Why do you raise such questions in your hearts? Which is easier, to say, "Your sins are forgiven you", or to say, "Stand up and walk"? But so that you may know that the Son of Man has authority on earth to forgive sins'—he said to the one who was paralysed - 'I say to you, stand up and take your bed and go to your home.' Immediately he stood up before them, took what he had been lying on, and went to his home, glorifying God. Amazement seized all of them, and they glorified God and were filled with awe, saying, 'We have seen strange things today.'

Painting: All in Relationship, 2001

Bart and Phil and Matt and me. I'm Mark. Not 'that' Mark, just Mark. Like Matt's not 'that' Matt either. We're not special and we're not claiming to be. Just happened to be us that did that thing. That day. We wouldn't even have done it if Stevo's mum hadn't gone the whole weeping and wailing thing on us. Didn't feel like we had a lot of choice after that. Anyway, just saying. Not big-noting ourselves. Just telling you what happened.

Anyway, going back. Stevo's one of us. We're just workers. One day here, six months there, depending on what's available. We get by. We have fun. We all grew up together, in each other's houses, doing dumb stuff. We look out for each other. We're mates.

One day we're working, picking olives, raking them out of trees. Bart's being an idiot and throwing olives at everyone. Sticking them up his nose, in his ears, just trying to get a laugh out of us. But it was hot and Stevo got narky with him, telling him pull his head in. Red rag to a bull. Bart starts chucking handfuls at Stevo, and Stevo loses it. He charges at Bart but slips on all the olives. He goes down like the wall of Jericho and just lies there. Well, the rest of us just crack up. We're rolling about the ground, shaking with laughter. Then Phil, always the sensible one of us, tells us to shut up. Stevo hasn't moved. He not laughing. He's not doing anything.

We go over to where he's lying, and we can tell something's not right. Stevo can be a pain, but he doesn't hold a grudge. He can take a joke. Matt and me, we reach down to grab his hands to pull him up but Phil, Phil screams at us to stop. He can see something we can't. Stevo's trying to talk. He's got tears in his eyes. "Get up you big idiot", says Bart, helpfully. He doesn't move a muscle. He can't move a muscle. He can't move. He's smashed something. Inside. When we made a stretcher out of branches to get him home, and lifted him gently on to it, we saw the rock. Under his back. Not a big rock. Big enough. Smashed something.

Took him back to his parents and they just looked at us. His dad went real quiet. His mum started to cry, but without any sound at all. They knew. They knew he wasn't going to get up. Ever. We didn't understand that then. We were indestructible.

We visited every day. At first. Then every few days. Work, you know. Then every week. Then....when we could. Except Bart. He felt real bad. Couldn't face Stevo' s folks. He went real quiet and he stopped making jokes. He was feeling it. Thought it was his fault. We told him it was just dumb luck, but he wasn't having that. He felt real bad.

Stevo could talk, but he didn't say much. It wasn't good. Nothing was good anymore.

Then that day. Whole town buzzing. Some visiting Rabbi. Bloke called Jesus. People going loopy all over the shop. I'm as religious as the next bloke but....well, this was a bit weird. All sorts of talk about stuff that just wasn't possible - unless God had actually come to town. Like that was going to happen.

So, I knock off work and walk over to Stevo's. Hadn't seen him for days and I was feeling a bit rubbish about myself because of that. I never knew what to say. I always felt...I don't know...kind of uncomfortable around him those days. But I knew he liked it when we dropped by. Sometimes he'd ask about my day, and he didn't seem to mind that I just rambled on. Better than nothing I suppose. Which is what he had. Nothing.

We were just sitting there when his mum comes in and starts crying and talking and begging me to take him to this Jesus bloke. She says that he's going to heal him and make him well. Says he's been doing it everywhere and that God has sent him here for Stevo. I said that I didn't think this Jesus actually knew about Stevo and she says – in no uncertain terms - to mind my manners and that God knows about Stevo, and God talks to Jesus and God told him about Stevo and that's why he's here. So, I ask why Jesus hasn't come over, if that's why he's here and...well, that wasn't the smartest question I've ever asked, and she goes into full meltdown mode, and I can't really understand what she's saying but I can tell she really wants me to get Stevo to Jesus.

I round up the lads. Phil and Matt are no problem, but Bart doesn't want to do it. He doesn't want to see Stevo. I tell him to man up and get a life and think about what Stevo's going through and how, if there's a one in a million chance of something good happening then he owes that to Stevo and…you get the picture. I guilt him into coming.

We carry Stevo on the stretcher. Bart's saying nothing. Stevo just looks scared. Phil's being practical. Matt's doing what he's told. I'm talking to fill the silence. When we get to the place where Jesus is at, it's mayhem. Twenty, thirty deep around the front of the house. No-one's letting us through. They're all here for something and that something doesn't make way for Stevo. We retreat. I think about Stevo's mum and I'm not happy.

Matt takes off. I think he's legged it and won't be back, but five minutes and he's yelling at us to pick up Stevo and follow his lead. He takes us around the back of the house where nobody's waiting. No doors, no windows, no point. I seriously want to whack him. Then he points at the roof, and I don't want to whack him anymore. I want to kiss him. But I don't. Of course I don't!

It wasn't easy getting Stevo up onto the roof. It wasn't easy making a hole in that roof. It was really embarrassing when we all stuck our heads through the hole, and we see Jesus all covered in dust from the mess we'd made and everyone else looking at us like we'd taken a piss in the temple sanctuary. I knew we'd cop it tomorrow. But we hadn't come for us, and whatever happened tomorrow was tomorrow's business.

We had ropes and we started to lower Stevo into the room. It had gone super quiet. The Jesus bloke – I knew it was him because he was the only one there who looked even vaguely like he knew what was going on – just watched. Stevo was terrified. There was nothing he could do, and we were taking the tiniest bit of dignity he had left and throwing him to the wolves. He was crying again, and I felt like a dog.

We lowered him as gently as we could onto the ground, then we just hung over the whole gathering, our ugly mugs sticking through the ceiling. And Jesus looks at Stevo. And Stevo looks at Jesus. Probably just a few seconds but it felt like eternity.

Then Jesus kneels down next to him and says, 'Friend, your sins are forgiven you.' That's all. Nothing else. And I think that Stevo's mum's not going to be real happy about that. I can see us taking him home and saying, 'It's all good Mrs Stevo, he's still totally wrecked but his sins are forgiven'. That was going to go well. Not that Stevo doesn't have a few things that need forgiving. Like the time he told Matt's sister, Miriam, that I wanted to marry her – when we were 9!! Idiot. And...well...a few other things too. But who doesn't?

I was just telling the boys to start hoisting him up when someone speaks up. The place was full of the religious men, not just from our town but all sorts I'd never seen. Important looking men who were looking at us as if we were dirt. To be fair, they were looking at Jesus like that too. Anyway, this bloke says, 'Who is this who is speaking blasphemies? Who can forgive sins but God alone?', and there's a whole lot of murmurings of agreement. Like they wanted to make Jesus look stupid.

But Jesus didn't even bat an eyelid. He comes straight back at them, 'Why do you raise such questions in your hearts? Which is easier, to say, "Your sins are forgiven you", or to say, "Stand up and walk"? But so that you may know that the Son of Man has authority on earth to forgive sins, I say to you, stand up and take your bed and go to your home.'

And I was so angry at him. At Jesus. It was my fault Stevo was there, but he was just making fun of him now. Yeah mate, get up and walk. Why not?

Then I looked at Stevo, and there was this weird gleam in his eyes. Not tears. Not anything I'd ever seen before. And we watched him get up. And we watched him pick up that stretcher. And we watched him look Jesus in the eye, and nod, and walk out through a crowd that just dissolved in front of him. Then I couldn't see anything anymore, because I was crying too hard. Not just me either. All of us, raining tears on all those important religious blokes, and not being able to stop.

REFLECT:

What are your responses to the story? How does the story change, seeing the situation from the perspective of the friends? Are there things you have understood about the character, or the encounter, that were not in your thinking before? What is your emotional response? Are there things that make you angry? Or sad? Or happy? Or.....? Does this imaginative retelling ring true to you? Why? Why not?

QUOTE:

"Dear Child of God, I write these words because we all experience sadness, we all come at times to despair, and we all lose hope that the suffering in our lives and in the world will ever end. I want to share with you my faith and my understanding that this suffering can be transformed and redeemed. There is no such thing as a totally hopeless case. Our God is an expert at dealing with chaos, with brokenness, with all the worst that we can imagine. God created order out of disorder, cosmos out of chaos, and God can do so always, can do so now - in our personal lives and in our lives as nations, globally. ... Indeed, God is transforming the world now - through us - because God loves us."
Desmond Tutu[1]

AN ABM RESPONSE:

Much of ABM and AID's work is centred on justice-based, practical outcomes that respond to the needs expressed by communities round the world. That being said, our Church to Church program continues to support theological training, mentoring and discovery in PNG, Africa and Australia. Of huge importance to the church is the work being done by indigenous people around the country as they help us to understand the heart of reconciliation, the long history of God with their peoples prior to white invasion, and how we might truly come to worship God in a way that recognises and embraces 'country'. Forgiveness, reconciliation and the ongoing living out of the Gospel of inclusion continue to change, challenge and offer hope to the world.

---

1   God Has a Dream: A Vision of Hope for Our Time, Doubleday, 2004.

DISCUSS:

Stories of miraculous healings are as wonderful as they are rare. The joy of healing is very real, and it is not our place to stand in the way of what God does – or to direct it. But these stories can also be used as vehicles of unspeakable damage. Huge numbers of people have been shamed, blamed and abused because they have not been able to claim a miraculous healing. They have been told that they 'didn't pray hard enough', or that they, 'obviously don't really believe'. Or they have been cruelly shunned because those who prayed for them feel badly that their prayers were inadequate. This type of behaviour is a form of spiritual abuse and must be called out for what it is. There is nothing loving about blaming someone for not being healed. There is nothing admirable about failing to see the incredible courage, strength, and faith of those who live with their brokenness and remain both hopeful and resilient.

Our lived experience tells us that miracles can happen, but they are not ours to control. Our lived experience tells us that pain is a reality many of us have no choice but to live with. So, what is going on here? If the healings are 'signs' of the broader work of the kingdom, what can we take away?

In this wonderful but strange encounter, even Jesus fails to act in the way we might expect. A paralysed man is let down through the ceiling and Jesus resolutely forgives his sins. Doesn't heal him. Not then. Not at first. Not even with his friends looking down, after some heroic work to get him there. Instead of a round of applause from the watching religious leaders, there's a swift accusation of blasphemy. And then the blinding light. The sign. Jesus explains that the miracle has already occurred but that they neither saw it nor understood it. It is, in fact, completely unacceptable to the religious leaders who have come to listen to Jesus. The miracle is that the 'Stevo' of our story did walk away, but he walked away healed. Forgiven. That's the commonplace miracle that we so often ignore.

The church and the world are full of people just like us. Like Matt and Bart and Phil and Mark. Like Jane and Clare and Sasha and Anna. We carry around a deep sense of inadequacy before God. Many of us carry secret hurts and guilts. Many of us have regrets that cripple us and infect every new relationship we attempt. And each morning we are offered the commonplace miracle of forgiveness. If only we can hear and understand.

The crowd will always want clear and practical outcomes. But the crowd is made up of individuals who all need forgiveness. Because – and we know this at the very deepest level – forgiveness frees us, in mind, body and soul, to become whole and human and hopeful again. Forgiveness opens the door that can allow us back to ourselves and our families and our communities because we are no longer ashamed, and we no longer feel judged. It is not always a straightforward path in every case and – like other miracles – forgiveness can and must never be forced or coerced. Freely and wholeheartedly given, it is the seed of resurrected hope.

Forgiveness may also lead us back, fuelled by gratitude and trust, into the arms of God. Forgiveness 'heals'. And that is why we continue to proclaim the Gospel and to offer to a cynical world, and an uncertain church, the message of transformational love.

The message of forgiveness is the greatest gift – and the most ordinary miracle – the church has to offer. It can even be given when it has not been requested – as Jesus does in this story – because the act of forgiveness can potentially free both parties involved, giver and receiver. It allows for new beginnings. The message – the offer - of forgiveness remains a living testament of God's profligate, irrational, mysterious, generous and wholehearted willingness to welcome God's children – and all of God's creation - back into the fullness of eternal oneness.

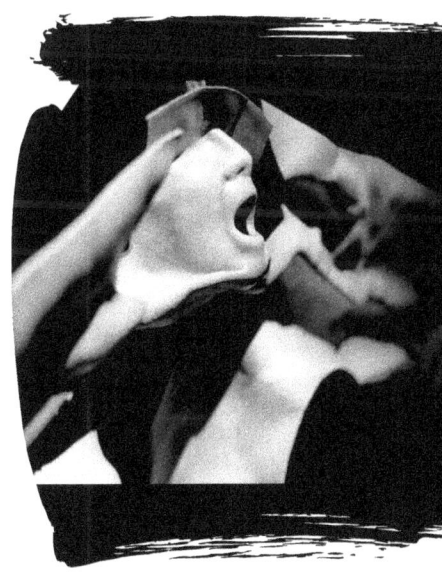

Painting: Pieces of Wholeness - Room for You 1986

QUESTIONS:

1. INDIVIDUAL

- Without telling others what forgiveness is, share what the results of forgiveness (or the lack of it) has meant in your own life.
- Why might it be difficult to forgive?
- Is a sense of God's forgiveness real to you? Why? Why not?

2. COMMUNITY

- In which areas of our community life might the message of forgiveness help heal long-standing wounds and fissures?
- Where might our community seek forgiveness and where might we offer it?

3. CHURCH

- Do you think that we place much emphasis on the message and offer of forgiveness in our worship and shared life? Why? Why not?
- Where might our church seek forgiveness and where might we offer it?

NOTES:

ADDITIONAL CREATIVE RESOURCES

Song: The Porter's Gate - Little Things With Great Love

Google it or go to: https://youtu.be/pm5VQAxdMrc

The Porter's Gate is a collective of fifty-plus songwriters, musicians, scholars, pastors, and music industry professionals from a variety of Christian worship traditions and cultural backgrounds, making music for churches.

Poetry or Prose: **Father, Forgive** *by Malcolm Guite*[2]

Father forgive, and so forgiveness flows;
Flows from the very wound our hatred makes,
Flows through the taunts, the curses and the blows,
Flows through our wasted world, a healing spring,
Welling and cleansing, washing all the marks
Away, the scores and scars of every wrong.

Forgiveness flows to where we need it most:
Right in the pit and smithy of our sin,
Just where the dreadful nails are driven in,
Just where our woundedness has done its worst.
We know your cry of pain should be a curse,
Yet turn to you and find we have been blessed.
We know not what we do, but Heaven knows
For every sin on earth, forgiveness flows.

---

[2] From Parable & Paradox (pg69) by Malcolm Guite, Canterbury Press (2016) https://malcolmguite.wordpress.com/

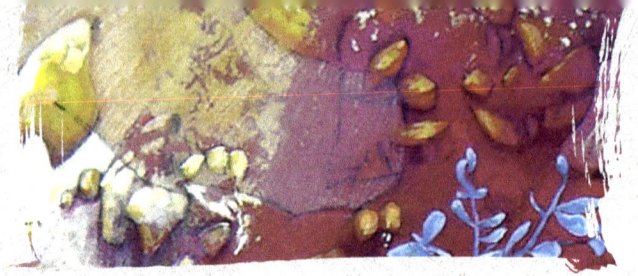

MARK 5:25-34

Now there was a woman who had been suffering from haemorrhages for twelve years. She had endured much under many physicians, and had spent all that she had; and she was no better, but rather grew worse. She had heard about Jesus, and came up behind him in the crowd and touched his cloak, for she said, 'If I but touch his clothes, I will be made well.' Immediately her haemorrhage stopped; and she felt in her body that she was healed of her disease. Immediately aware that power had gone forth from him, Jesus turned about in the crowd and said, 'Who touched my clothes?' And his disciples said to him, 'You see the crowd pressing in on you; how can you say, "Who touched me?"' He looked all round to see who had done it. But the woman, knowing what had happened to her, came in fear and trembling, fell down before him, and told him the whole truth. He said to her, 'Daughter, your faith has made you well; go in peace, and be healed of your disease.'

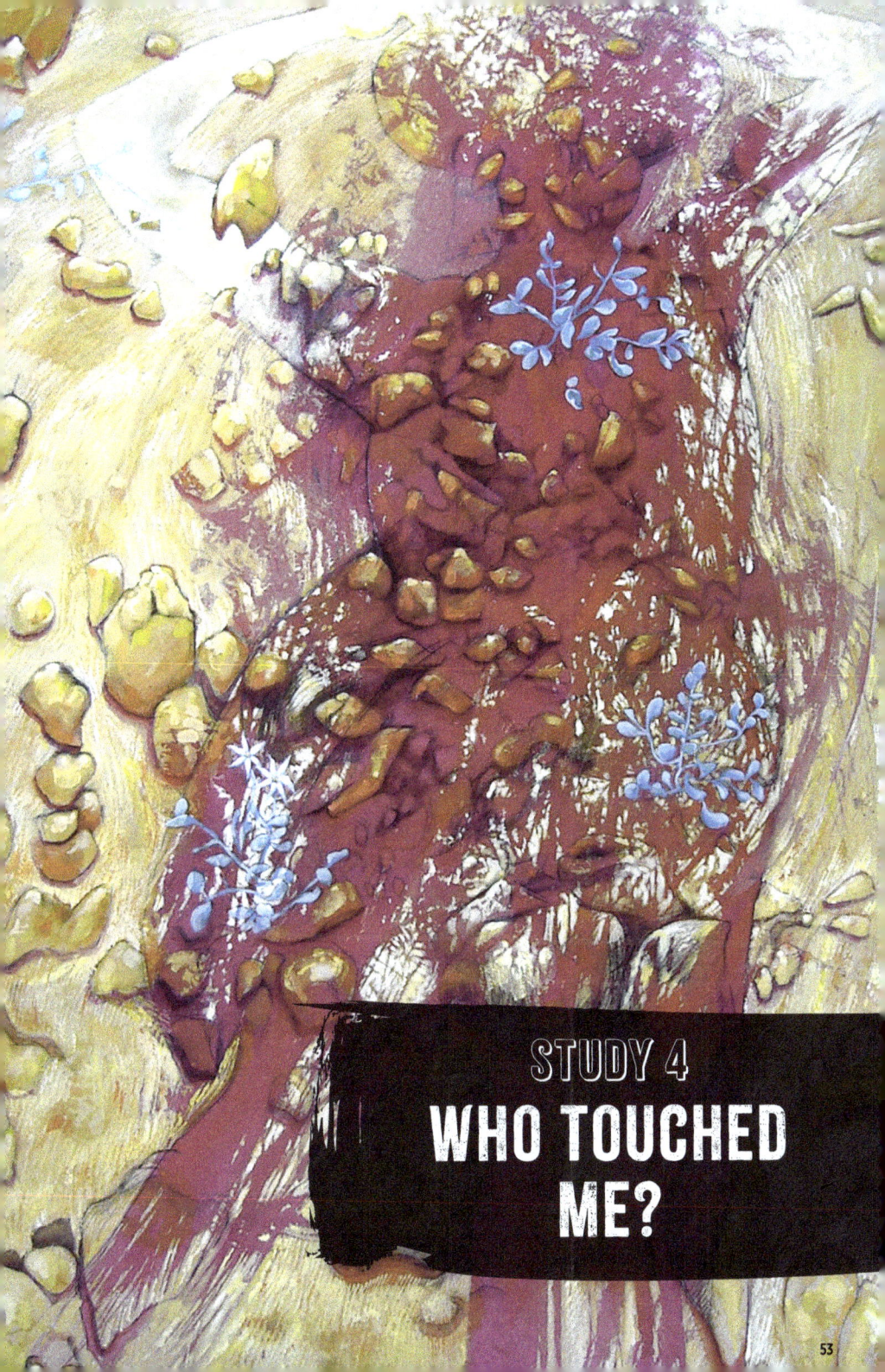

To be a woman. To bleed. To become invisible.

If people say that I have lived in my memories, perhaps that is because, in my memories, I existed. I was seen. I was loved.

My childhood was joy upon joy. My mother's raucous laugh and my father's stern but gentle gaze. Teasing my brothers, corralling my sisters, roaming the streets with packs of children looking for small adventures.

Then the blood came. I was proud. I was a woman. By then I already knew who I would marry. Benjamin was four years older than me, and our parents had arranged the match. Some girls did far worse. Old men. Far away men. Cruel men. They talked of running away, killing themselves. Not me. I felt blessed. Benjamin was handsome. He was kind. He was quiet and respectful. He genuinely seemed to like me.

I was pretty. Everyone said so, and you know when people are just saying it and when they mean it. I caught him looking. I caught his eye. I was so full of the future I almost burst.

The monthly pain, the inconvenience, the being shut away and unclean. Almost every woman endured it. Some better, some worse. For me it was worse. But it was worst of all if you didn't have it. My life was changing but it was rolling forward in ways that made my breath catch in my throat.

We were married, and it was strange and beautiful and exciting and so, so good. We were happy, our families close and always food on the table. Each bright morning sang to us of peace and each evening sky whispered of rest and embraces.

The blood stopped. The baby kicked. Benjamin brought me dates and rubbed my feet. My mother came each day and spoke of what was to come. I wasn't scared.

The birth was like a kicking mule and burning brand. I cried and I screamed and I bled. I battled the dark angel of pain and I lost. The squalling life at my breast, the onset of milk, the rush of love, the victory.

The bleeding. The bleeding. The bleeding.

Irregular. Ongoing. Uncontrollable. Unclean. Never free long enough to become clean. The looks on the faces of my family. My husband. The fight to keep my child with me. The deep, rending grief of losing. The same walls every day. The loss of laughter. Touch. Conversation. Company. The loss.

The bleeding.

The days turned to weeks and the weeks turned to months. The months became years. Eleven years. Benjamin would not come to me. He was devout. Still kind, he sought every doctor, every healer, every mad itinerant holy one. He begged them. They came and went. Came with promises and prayers and potions. Left with our money, blood on their hands.

I watched my child grow, living for the days I sometimes had when I could emerge and hold him. I thanked God he was a boy. He would never know this shame.

I learned tricks to cover the bleeding. I walked the streets, but no-one met my eye. What sort of sin had I committed that had cursed our family in this way? I learned to despair quietly and to weep without sound. It was easier to stay home. To give in. To disappear.

The noise from the streets lifted me from blackness. A knock at the closed shutter. Benjamin's voice. "It's Jesus". Who? "Jesus. The Rabbi, the healer, the miracle worker. Come. Quickly."

Better to stay home. Better to disappear. My heart was not broken. It was crushed.

"Come, Veronica. Maybe he...maybe...". Maybe the stars would fall, and the sky turn black. One more charlatan. One more nail.

"He will be here soon. Please, Veronica. For me. For the boy."

For them. Fresh rags and new bindings. For my loves. Dress for the marketplace. To slap despair back. Veil in place. To prove I am alive. Don't draw attention.

There was no question which one he was. The air vibrated on the note of hope. I was transfixed. To me he was a beacon, lit from within, and as I walked the crowd simply parted. Power surged from him. Others didn't seem to notice. I had long ago run out of prayers, run out of words. I knew that all I needed was to touch him, his clothes, his sandals. My hand reached out. Flesh on fabric. Rapture. Gasping intake of breath, as if I'd been underwater for a decade. Slow burning, surging flood of tears.

No blood. No blood. Dry, and clean, and over.

No-one noticed. I was invisible. The crowd moved on. Then he turned. "Who touched me?" They laughed. Who hadn't?

"Who touched me?" Eyes on me. Fixed. Understanding. I knelt. I confessed.

"Daughter, your faith has healed you. Go in peace and be freed from your suffering."

He took my hand. Dared to touch me. He raised me to my feet. He set me free.

No blood.

Three years now and there has been nothing but the normal blood. I am like the others. There has been no blood now for five months. Life stirs.

Benjamin brings me dates. Eli will be fifteen soon and he will marry. We are still learning each other, after all those years of separation. His children will play at my feet, and I will cook for them and teach them to greet each morning as a gift. I will speak to them of Jesus, who the Elders say is dead - but who they desperately fear is alive. Jesus, who bled. We have learned much of what he said, and Benjamin and I break the bread and share the wine with others foolish enough to hope.

There is so much bleeding in the world. There is so much healing to be done.

REFLECT:

What are your responses to the story? How does the story change, seeing the situation from the perspective of the haemorrhaging woman? Are there things you have understood about the character, or the encounter, that were not in your thinking before? What is your emotional response? Are there things that make you angry? Or sad? Or happy? Or.....? Does this imaginative retelling ring true to you? Why? Why not?

QUOTE:

"I remember when we parted there was an awkward moment when the severity of my situation and our unfamiliarity with each other left us with no words, and in a gesture that I'm sure was completely unconscious, he placed his hand over his heart for just a second as a flicker of empathetic anguish crossed his face. It sliced right through me. It cut through the cloud I was living in and let the plain day pour its balm upon me. It was, I am sure, one of those moments when we enact and reflect a mercy and mystery that are greater than we are, when the void of God and the love of God, incomprehensible pain and the peace that passeth understanding, come together in a simple human act. We stood for a minute in the aftermath, not talking, and then went our suddenly less separate ways."

Christian Wiman[1]

---

1   My Bright Abyss: Meditation of a Modern Believer, Farrar Straus Giroux (1 June 2014)

AN ABM RESPONSE:

One of the greatest risks to human health is a lack of clean water. For decades, ABM, with the support of the Australian Government, has been working with communities in many countries, as they have planned and implemented sustainable, locally designed solutions to a lack of clean water. The Water, Sanitation and Hygiene (WASH) projects in Myanmar are one example of this. Clean water means personal hygiene, safe cooking and cleaning, sanitation improvements and the ability to rehydrate without inviting disease. These projects are not what most people would describe as miraculous...but the results are.

DISCUSS:

Many of us are profoundly uncomfortable with illness – especially 'private' illnesses that touch on the taboo areas of life. Those with chronic illnesses and pain, often become outsiders in our communities, feeling both misunderstood and, sometimes, shunned. This is even more true in certain cultures across the planet, cultures that still equate illness with past or 'sinful' behaviours.

"What have they done to deserve this?" is a question we still ask when we are baffled by what can seem unjust suffering. We may intellectually know that we are not talking about a 'cause and effect' situation, but we still use the phrases that indicate we are not far, historically, from the time when our own culture was quick to shun the ill.

We are often shocked by illness or accident happening within families we know and love. "What a shame, she was such a lovely girl too – with such a bright future ahead of her". "It's too bad, I thought he'd go on to great things". Somehow, disease seems foreign to those who live in the light. But, of course, it is not. Nor is a tragedy that befalls the rich and beautiful any more or less important than one that befalls the poor. Our own lives help us to know this. Things happen. We live in a broken world. Beautiful, but broken in ways that can break us.

It is no longer common practice to shut up the mentally and physically ill in places removed from the rest of us. Partly this is because we now have a far greater understanding of the underlying causes of many illnesses, and we do not allocate blame and shame to those already suffering. Partly it is because the example Jesus set us, of going to those who suffered - touching those who were untouchable – has helped us understand a new way of being in the world. St Francis of Assisi, great saint of the created world and lover of those on the edge, has also inspired many, including the current Pope.

In this story from the Gospels, Jesus once more sees and recognises faith and hope, and responds with both cure and healing. The illness is gone, and the woman is restored to those she loves. The missional signals of healthy individuals living within healthy communities once again flashes across the pages of the Gospels. Our own calling is to follow and reflect the work and concerns of Jesus into a broken world. Every step we take towards those experiencing ostracism because of illness or fear, is a step that is witnessed by others, perhaps encouraging them to lessen the gaps that exist between people.

Every so often, we must take stock of our lives, our churches and our communities. Are we walking towards those who need us? Are we watching with interest? Are we stepping away?

QUESTIONS:

1. INDIVIDUAL

- Have you ever experienced an illness that has driven you away from others – or others away from you? How did that feel? Did you sense God's presence with you – or not?

- Have you experienced the ministry of others when you have been ill? Has that helped to strengthen your faith in the body of Christ?

2. COMMUNITY

- How do you reflect on the recent and ongoing Covid pandemic? Were our early responses the right ones? How quickly did stigma arise around those who had the disease? Was blame allocated? Were you aware of the voice of the church in the public debate?

- What diseases remain stigmatised in our community? Remember the AIDS scares? Not so long ago, Lepers were sent to islands. What are the untouchable diseases of our time? How do we influence community responses to both legitimate and unreasonable fears.

3. CHURCH

- Much of the hospital and medical system we now take for granted rose from a Christian response to universal suffering and the understanding that all people are worthy of care. What role does the/ our church now play in the care of the ill?

- What is the power of prayer in healing? Have a respectful but honest discussion of the views and experience within the group.

NOTES:

Song: The Porter's Gate - Daughters of Zion
(feat. Casey J & Urban Doxology)

Google it or go to: https://youtu.be/_zh9JgvRQsM

The Porter's Gate is a collective of fifty-plus songwriters, musicians, scholars, pastors, and music industry professionals from a variety of Christian worship traditions and cultural backgrounds, making music for churches.

Poetry or Prose: **A Prayer of Awed Thanks for Nurses**
by Brian Doyle[2]

Witnesses, attendants, bringers of peace; brilliant technical machinists; selfless cleaners of all liquids no matter how horrifying; deft finders of veins when no veins seem available; soothers and calmers and amusers; tireless and patient and tender souls; brisk and efficient when those are the tools to keep despair at bay; those with prayers in their mouths as their patients slide gently through the mysterious gate, never to return in a form like the shrivelled still one in the bed; feeders and teasers, mercies and singers; they who miss nothing with their eyes and ears and fingers and hearts; they who are not saluted and celebrated and worshipped as they ought to be; they who are the true administrators of hospitals and clinics, for it is they who have their holy hands on the brows and bruises of the broken and frightened; they who carry the new infants to their sobbing exhausted thrilled mothers; they who must carry the news of damage and death to the family in the waiting room; they whom You know, each and every one, glorious and lovely in their greens and blues and rainbow clothing; they who are You in every tender touch and quiet friendly gentle murmured remark; they who are the best of us; bless them always and always, Mercy; for they are the clan of calm and the tribe of tender, and I bow in thanks for them. And so: amen.

---

2   A Book of Uncommon Prayer - 100 Celebrations of the Miracle & Muddle of the Ordinary, Sorin Books 2014

LUKE 19:1-10

He entered Jericho and was passing through it. A man was there named Zacchaeus; he was a chief tax collector and was rich. He was trying to see who Jesus was, but on account of the crowd he could not, because he was short in stature. So he ran ahead and climbed a sycamore tree to see him, because he was going to pass that way. When Jesus came to the place, he looked up and said to him, "Zacchaeus, hurry and come down; for I must stay at your house today." So he hurried down and was happy to welcome him. All who saw it began to grumble and said, "He has gone to be the guest of one who is a sinner." Zacchaeus stood there and said to the Lord, "Look, half of my possessions, Lord, I will give to the poor; and if I have defrauded anyone of anything, I will pay back four times as much." Then Jesus said to him, "Today salvation has come to this house, because he too is a son of Abraham. For the Son of Man came to seek out and to save the lost."

Painting: Pastel landscape

The first elbow caught me just below the eye, opening a cut. You know how wounds to the head bleed! I wasn't angry. Not at that point. I just thought it was one of the prices I pay for being slightly shorter than others. Slightly. Elbow height. Alright, a lot! Shorter. It's hardly my fault.

I'd pushed my way into the crowd. I'd calculated the risks. I always do. That's why I'm good at what I do. Most of the time people assume I'm a child, and just let me through. Not this time. I'd been spotted.

The second elbow wasn't an elbow. Probably a knee. It winded me. I have no idea whose knee. I think it broke a rib. It was mayhem. The whole crowd was struggling forward for a glimpse of Jesus, and there was more than the usual share of pushing and shoving, whining and shouting. But they knew I was there. And they took their chance. The tax-collector. Vulnerable. Alone. Why not? Why not indeed?

When my head went down and my hands to my knees, a couple of fists cuffed the back of my head. Then one of them kicked my feet from under me. I went down hard. Seriously, I thought I was dead. I thought they'd just trample me. The irony of it! All of us, trying to catch a glimpse of the great healer, and here they were, taking revenge and putting the boot in.

There was dust in my eyes, smeared to red mud as I tried to wipe the blood away. Dust in my throat. Dust up my nose, in my ears. Such shame. Again. The daily ritual of being hated, finally made flesh. Bruised flesh.

Uri parted the crowd. People always move back when he approaches them. They pay up too. He doesn't have to ask. He picked me up and carried me out. They spat at his back. Wouldn't dare to his front. He's a foreigner and a slave. My slave. I don't fully understand why he's so loyal. He took me to the spring. Washed me down. Made sure I was making sense. Then he motioned me to follow.

We cut across town, not following the crowd. I assumed Jesus and his friends would head for the Synagogue. Uri knew better. Close to the market, he stopped and gestured to a tree. Me, the chief tax-collector, I was to climb a tree. I told him exactly what I thought of the idea. He shrugged. He sat.

I heard the crowd approaching. Heading in our direction. Jesus somewhere in the middle, surrounded by cries for help. Invitations. Abuse. Everyone was there. Celebrity! Love them or hate them, everyone wants a part of it. I looked at Uri. He crouched. Made a step with his hands. Just like my father used to when I was a child.

From the branches, I could see the roofs. I thought to myself that I must remember this. Easy to see what people are hiding, stored on their roofs, maybe not paying tax on. The sun was high, the white walls of the city glaring, the dust of the crowd hazing everything. The sound was like an onrushing Babel. Voice over voice, different languages, children, women, men. A rowdy, slow moving vortex of desperation, curiosity and self-interest. Much like any other day. So I thought.

I could see him, in glimpses, somewhere towards the front. His friends pushing people away, trying to make a straight path. Somehow, in the middle of it all he seemed calm. Or maybe determined. He looked like....a man. Not young. Not old. Not anything in particular. Then he looked up.

Not many people do. Look up. Mostly eyes down or darting around, looking for the sucker punch that'll take them out. Like I should have. But he looked up. Then he stopped. The crowd didn't. He was shunted forward another few body lengths. But he was still looking. At me. Then the crowd looked too. The laughter began. The hurled insults. The screamed accusations. The flow of angry, resentful vitriol. I didn't blame them. I collect the taxes of those who make their lives hard. Ha! Even if I collected taxes for the great King David, they'd still hate me. I collect taxes. Jesus was getting a generous earful of stories about my parentage and prospects. Then he spoke.

It's quite a voice. Cuts through. Not aggressive, but loud, clear and full of authority. He called for silence. He began to walk towards me. He came to the foot of the tree. He sat beside Uri, putting his arm around him. The crowd watched, perhaps expecting a punchline. Jesus whispered in Uri's ear. Uri turned his head to him and whispered back. I had never seen that before. Uri has no tongue. It was cut out by a previous owner. I don't know why. But he spoke to Jesus. Then Jesus stood.

"Zacchaeus, hurry and come down; for I must stay at your house today."

Dead silence. Then a few sniggers. Then silence. Uri helped me down. I was talking. Talking rubbish. Words spilling out in the shock of what was happening. The crowd was not happy, not happy at all. I just wanted to calm it all down. I don't know why I even said it. I hadn't even thought it before it was out of my mouth.

"Look, half of my possessions, Lord, I will give to the poor; and if I have defrauded anyone of anything, I will pay back four times as much."

My words fell into a well of silence. Everyone heard. If there was anyone more shocked than me, I'd be very surprised. Jesus looked at me again. There was the hint of a smile. The crowd started to spit again. Calling me a liar and a hypocrite. There were voices raised against Jesus too. We stood. Uri like a statue. Jesus, calm. Me, jittery and wincing. They muttered and dispersed.

At my house, I quickly hustled the servants into action. Water to wash. Food and wine. So much talk. I wasn't really used to guests. Of course, I had hosted parties – but not for friends. Jesus sat with Uri, talking quietly. Listening. Then he spoke with me. It was a good night. The best. It felt like family.

I couldn't sleep. I remembered what I had said. It terrified me. It would break me. Ruin me. I lit a lamp. I did the books. Both sets. Official and unofficial. It was worse than I had thought. Half – to give away half – would leave me with hardly more than I would need to repay the defrauded in the manner I had promised. Four times! This was madness. Uri watched me.

Then we began. Out into the darkness. Like thieves, but in reverse.

We knocked on doors. I explained. I apologised. I repaid. I left gifts. I stripped my warehouse.

The next morning there was a crowd at my front door. News travels swiftly. I set up table and continued. People took what I gave. Rarely a smile. Rarely any thanks. I had a black eye. My ribs hurt. Uri sat with me. Jesus sat with us. As midday approached, he stood. The crowd waiting. That voice again.

"Today salvation has come to this house because he too is a son of Abraham. For the Son of Man came to seek out and to save the lost."

Bewilderment. Suspicion. Laughter. Disquiet. Quiet.

We ate again. We spoke. Jesus left. Uri and I continued. It took us days.

I am ruined, and somehow happier. Everything I had promised has now been fulfilled.

The house is very empty. Very quiet. No guests. No laughter.

Last night, there was a knock at the door. When Uri opened it, there was no one. At his feet, some barley loaves. Some figs.

I wept.

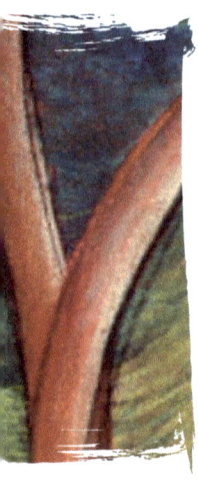

REFLECT:

What are your responses to the story? Why do you think Jesus took the risk of standing with Zacchaeus? Are there things you have understood about the character, or the encounter, that were not in your thinking before? What is your emotional response? Are there things that make you angry? Or sad? Or happy? Or.....? Does this imaginative retelling ring true to you? Why? Why not?

QUOTE:

"My lifetime of studying Jesus would lead me to summarize all of his teaching inside of two prime ideas: forgiveness and inclusion. Don't believe me; just go through the Gospels, story by story. It is rather self-evident. Forgiveness and inclusion are Jesus' "great themes." They are the practical name of love, and without forgiveness and inclusivity love is largely a sentimental valentine. They are also the two practices that most undercut human violence."

Fr Richard Rohr[1]

---

1   Fr. Richard Rohr is a globally recognized ecumenical teacher bearing witness to the universal awakening within Christian mysticism and the Perennial Tradition. He is a Roman Catholic Franciscan priest of the New Mexico Province and founder of the Center for Action and Contemplation (CAC) in Albuquerque, New Mexico.

AN ABM RESPONSE:

For decades, ABM has worked with our Partner, the Episcopal/Anglican Diocese of Jerusalem. In the land of Jesus' birth, racial and religious tensions run high, and peace seems an unlikely possibility. In the midst of these troubles, faithful Christians continue to live out lives of reconciliation, peacemaking and justice. They are often a forgotten minority, but their Archbishop, the Most Reverend Hosam Naoum says, "These ministries serve to sustain and strengthen our Christian presence as we teach respect and concern for all people, bringing hope to many, regardless of faith, where the light of hope is often dim. With a dwindling church membership due to emigration caused by local strife and economic hardship, the ministry here has more than the usual challenges. The maintenance of the historic Arab Christian presence, the "Living Stones," is vital therefore to the future stability of the region as we put our faith into action "loving our neighbours as ourselves."

Let us pray for those who witness and minister in the most hostile and dangerous places, refusing to bow the knee to injustice, but instead, proclaiming in word and deed the Gospel of inclusive love.

DISCUSS:

This isn't a story about a short man who is a bit ridiculous because he must climb a tree in order to see Jesus. It's not a kid's story. It's a story about radical transformation of the type that many of us hope for – even pray for – in our own lives. It's about honouring promises and being received as if you already had. It's about the public affirmation of the enemy who has promised to change. It's about the way Jesus seeks to challenge and change us in ways that will be uncomfortable but freeing.

> 'You have heard that it was said, "You shall love your neighbour and hate your enemy." But I say to you, Love your enemies and pray for those who persecute you, so that you may be children of your Father

in heaven; for he makes his sun rise on the evil and on the good, and sends rain on the righteous and on the unrighteous. For if you love those who love you, what reward do you have? Do not even the tax-collectors do the same? And if you greet only your brothers and sisters, what more are you doing than others? Do not even the Gentiles do the same? Be perfect, therefore, as your heavenly Father is perfect.
Matthew 5:43-48

Most of us love the idea of loving our enemies, but baulk at the prospect of actually doing so. There's a reason for this. It's difficult. Very difficult. It shouldn't be underestimated just how difficult. If we're brutally honest, it's hard enough loving the people we love. Love is complex and changeable. Love is deep and shallow. Love is practical and fantastic. Even knowing what love means eludes many of us.

Zacchaeus was unpopular. A scapegoat. Already physically different, he was also the agent of the powers of government and occupation. He was dishonest. He was unlovable. He was lost.

The fear of getting lost is visceral. It is felt not only in the mind but in the body. No-one wants to be lost. From the story of Hansel and Gretel to the regular news reports of people who have gone off-track in the Australian wilderness, that sense that we have wandered away from the place we belong and do not know how to get back is gut-wrenching. In the mind of almost everyone who has ever been lost, grows the hope, faint or certain, that someone is looking for you. That you will be found and restored.

This 'finding' is the work of Christ. Thus, it is the work of the church. We are not very good at it. Again, this is understandable. The real business of 'finding' involves the genuine exercise of love, courage, commitment, sacrifice and humility. Zacchaeus was 'found' by Jesus. He was saved. He was restored. He was brought home. His repentance took on very real and practical meaning. He was utterly changed. Is this not what we hope for in all who encounter Jesus. Is this not something we seek each day as we follow Jesus? The business of being 'found' is a lifelong experience.

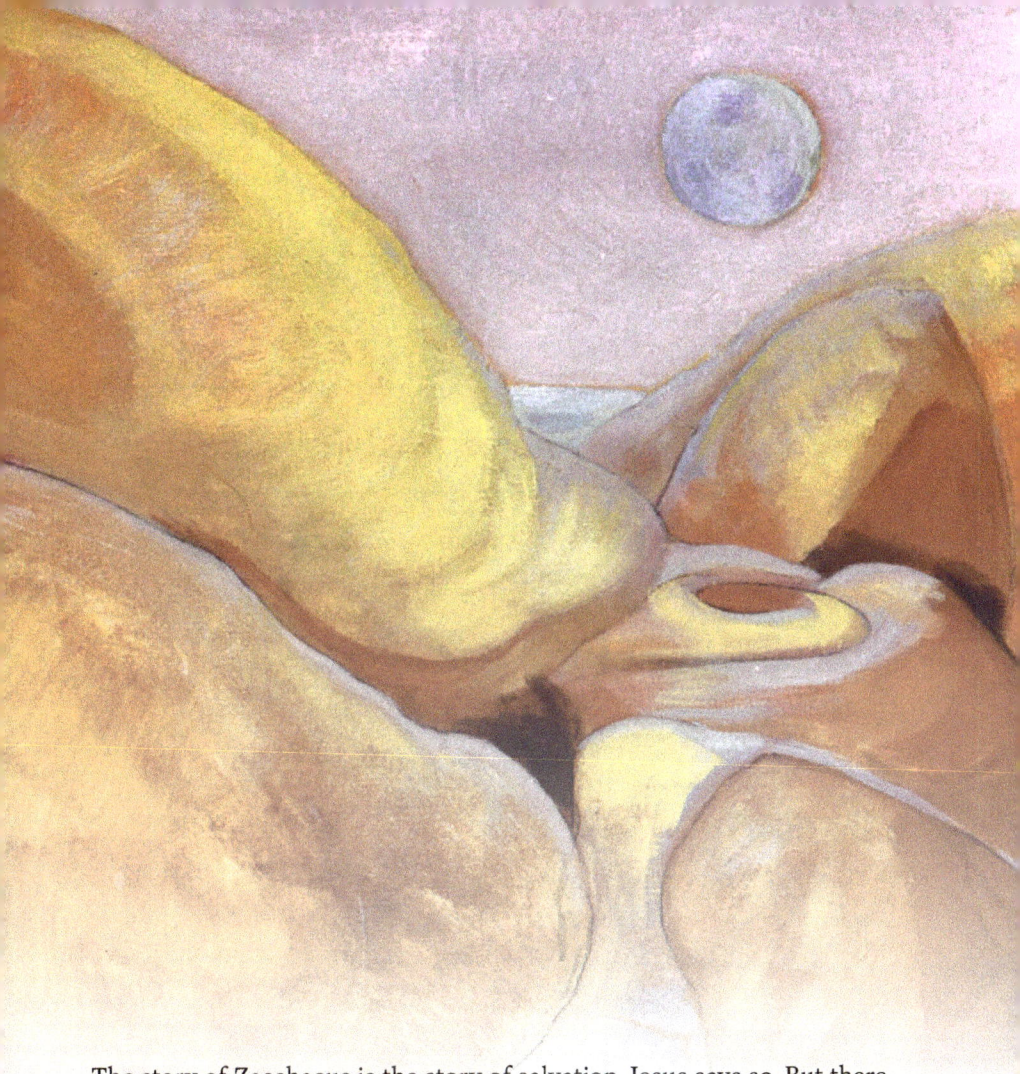

The story of Zacchaeus is the story of salvation. Jesus says so. But there are no recorded words of acknowledgement of faith or repentance – or even forgiveness. Yet, all those things happen within an encounter of generous and accepting love. The truly fertile ground of the church is the ground we stand on when we place ourselves next to the enemy, the scapegoat, the lost, the derided.

Once again, we see the results of the Gospel of inclusion. Jesus opening doors through which the lost can return home. May we too, be openers of doors and seekers of the lost. May we too remember the day-to-day moments when doors have been opened for us to walk through – and to come home.

Painting: Memory of Second Valley

QUESTIONS:

1. INDIVIDUAL

- Discuss what 'love' means. What is it? How is it expressed? Try and avoid cliches and be as honest as possible, not ignoring the difficulties.

- Have you experienced 'lostness'. Physically? Mentally? From family or community? Can you remember what it felt like? Have you experienced being 'found'?

- Have you ever stood with someone broadly condemned and excluded by others? Why? Has anyone stood by you when you needed support or felt unjustly treated?

2. COMMUNITY

- The high-tax/low-tax debate goes on at every election. We know that our taxes are funding the community services we expect and often complain are underfunded. What is a Christian response to the level and use of taxation? Have we a voice in the community?

- Certain professions are revered – and others scorned. Why? Is 'a fair day's work for a fair day's pay' indicative of the way our wages system works? How does our faith impact on the way we see justice and equality in the workplace?

3. CHURCH

- For many of us, we repent and seek forgiveness each week in the General Confession. Do you think repentance is an act of the mind and heart, or must it be shown in our actions as well?

- What does the church need to repent of in order to witness to Christ's great, inclusive love?

NOTES:

Painting: Icon of the Presence, on door

ADDITIONAL CREATIVE RESOURCES

Song: The Porter's Gate - The Zaccheaus Song

Google it or go to: https://youtu.be/WoNOe_zr2_0

Poetry or Prose: **Careful How You Pray** *by Steve Turner*[2]

Careful how you pray now.
You pray justice
come rollin' down
like a mighty river
and it might just come rollin'.
Might come rollin'
down your street.
Might come beatin'
up your walls.
Might come lickin'
'neath your door.

Might get wet. Might drown.

2 Poems – Steve Turner, Lion Publishing 2002

LAZARUS RAISED: JOHN 11:1-45

Now a certain man was ill, Lazarus of Bethany, the village of Mary and her sister Martha. Mary was the one who anointed the Lord with perfume and wiped his feet with her hair; her brother Lazarus was ill. So the sisters sent a message to Jesus, 'Lord, he whom you love is ill.' But when Jesus heard it, he said, 'This illness does not lead to death; rather it is for God's glory, so that the Son of God may be glorified through it.' Accordingly, though Jesus loved Martha and her sister and Lazarus, after having heard that Lazarus was ill, he stayed two days longer in the place where he was.

Then after this he said to the disciples, 'Let us go to Judea again.' The disciples said to him, 'Rabbi, the Jews were just now trying to stone you, and are you going there again?' Jesus answered, 'Are there not twelve hours of daylight? Those who walk during the day do not stumble, because they see the light of this world. But those who walk at night stumble, because the light is not in them.' After saying this, he told them,

'Our friend Lazarus has fallen asleep, but I am going there to awaken him.' The disciples said to him, 'Lord, if he has fallen asleep, he will be all right.' Jesus, however, had been speaking about his death, but they thought that he was referring merely to sleep. Then Jesus told them plainly, 'Lazarus is dead. For your sake I am glad I was not there, so that you may believe. But let us go to him.' Thomas, who was called the Twin, said to his fellow-disciples, 'Let us also go, that we may die with him.'

When Jesus arrived, he found that Lazarus had already been in the tomb for four days. Now Bethany was near Jerusalem, some two miles away, and many of the Jews had come to Martha and Mary to console them about their brother. When Martha heard that Jesus was coming, she went and met him, while Mary stayed at home. Martha said to Jesus, 'Lord, if you had been here, my brother would not have died. But even now I know that God will give you whatever you ask of him.' Jesus said to her, 'Your brother will rise again.' Martha said to him, 'I know that he will rise again in the resurrection on the last day.' Jesus said to her, 'I am the resurrection and the life. Those who believe in me, even though they die, will live, and everyone who lives and believes in me will never die. Do you believe this?' She said to him, 'Yes, Lord, I believe that you are the Messiah, the Son of God, the one coming into the world.'

When she had said this, she went back and called her sister Mary, and told her privately, 'The Teacher is here and is calling for you.' And when she heard it, she got up quickly and went to him. Now Jesus had not yet come to the village, but was still at the place where Martha had met him. The Jews who were with her in the house, consoling her, saw Mary get up quickly and go out. They followed her because they thought that she was going to the tomb to weep there. When Mary came where Jesus was and saw him, she knelt at his feet and said to him, 'Lord, if you had been here, my brother would not have died.' When Jesus saw her weeping, and the Jews who came with her also weeping, he was greatly disturbed in spirit and deeply moved. He said, 'Where have you laid him?' They said to him, 'Lord, come and see.' Jesus began to weep. So the Jews said, 'See how he loved him!' But some of them said, 'Could not he who opened the eyes of the blind man have kept this man from dying?'

Then Jesus, again greatly disturbed, came to the tomb. It was a cave, and a stone was lying against it. Jesus said, 'Take away the stone.' Martha, the sister of the dead man, said to him, 'Lord, already there is a stench because he has been dead for four days.' Jesus said to her, 'Did I not tell you that if you believed, you would see the glory of God?' So they took away the stone. And Jesus looked upwards and said, 'Father, I thank you for having heard me. I knew that you always hear me, but I have said this for the sake of the crowd standing here, so that they may believe that you sent me.' When he had said this, he cried with a loud voice, 'Lazarus, come out!' The dead man came out, his hands and feet bound with strips of cloth, and his face wrapped in a cloth. Jesus said to them, 'Unbind him, and let him go.'

Many of the Jews therefore, who had come with Mary and had seen what Jesus did, believed in him.

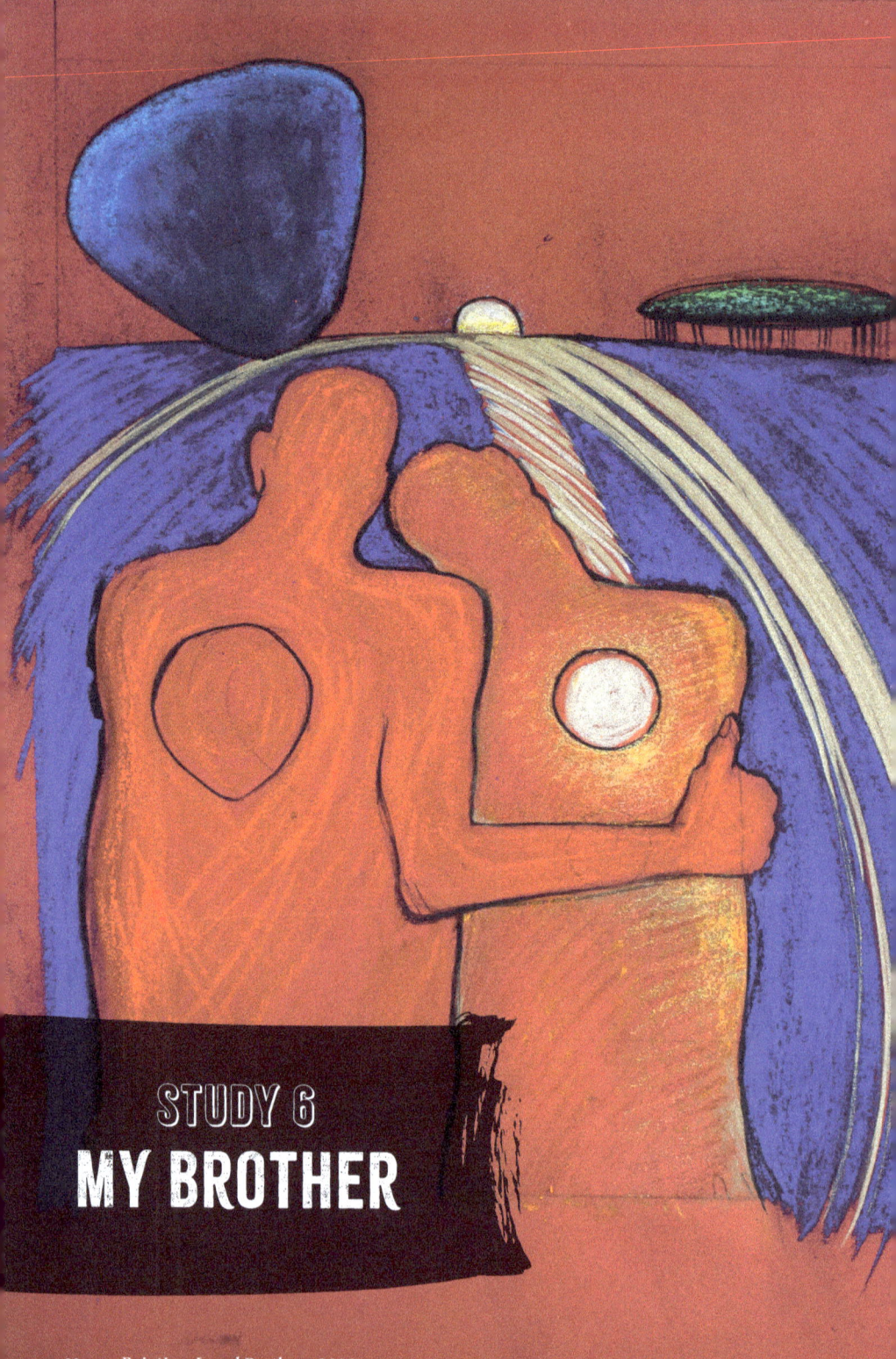

STUDY 6
MY BROTHER

Painting: Loved Brothers, 2023

He was dead, and he is alive again. That's two now. Both of my favourite men.

Of course, Lazarus – my brother - was first, but both were traumatic. Days of waiting, fearing the worst. Hoping against hope. Giving up. Rewriting our world and then having to scratch that all out and begin a new reality.

Lazarus was born long after Mary and me. Our mother was too old. The birth was difficult. We lost her and we got Lazarus. She would have been happy that he made it. She'd always wanted a son.

From the start, he struggled. He was small and weak at first, but soon he gained strength, the wet-nurse shepherding him through those early months. Then he was slow to walk, and slower to talk, and we began to see who he would become. Not what. Who. Right from the start, he was – and remains – the happiest, most loving, kindest man I've ever known. Mary and I love him for all he's done for us. Our little brother. The head of our house.

Our father did not live many years after the birth. Just long enough to make it clear how disappointed he was. Lazarus was not the son he wanted. I'm not sure he ever held him again, after it became clear. Lazarus would never grow up to be like other men. People said he was afflicted, broken, wrong. We said he was blessed. Our father would not see the blessing. He died, angry with God – and with himself. He was not a bad man. He simply couldn't see the gift. Lazarus, of course, inherited everything. He was the man. Or, at that stage, the boy. Mary and I became his guides – and he, our protector. He gave us our lives.

Lazarus learnt to run and dance and sing. He was not treated well by some children, but he never held a grudge. Adults who weren't scared of him, loved him. He was gentle with animals. He learned some words and he attended the synagogue. His faith in God was always strong. He did not insist that Mary and I marry. I doubt he even thought about it, so we did not. We ran his household, as many women run many households. Not everyone was happy with the arrangement, but we didn't care.

The first time Jesus came through Bethany, we took Lazarus to see him. It was big news. The moment Lazarus saw Jesus, he changed. He simply stopped dead and stared. Then he walked through the crowd until he was toe to toe with Jesus. The laughing began, of course. The cat-calls. Then Lazarus spoke.

"I know you, Jesus", he said. And Jesus replied, "And I know you, Lazarus". Then they embraced, as if they were brothers, and Lazarus took his hand and led him to us. Again, he spoke, "This is my friend, Jesus. He will stay with us". It remains the closest he has ever come to demanding anything. That's when it began. Jesus always stayed with us. The uncharitable and the gossips always said it was because of Mary and me, but that's not true. I like to think he always wanted to see us too. I know he did. But he always came to see Lazarus. They would walk and play and sing together. No-one else could get Jesus to relax so much. They loved each other. We loved Jesus because he loved our brother. Before we believed in him, we loved him.

Jesus saw exactly what we saw. No, that's not true. Jesus saw even more than we could see. In Lazarus he met someone pure of heart and full of the wonder of God. He always spoke to Lazarus as if he were the equal of anyone. They would talk long into the night. He did not speak down to him. He never left him out. Where Jesus was, when he was with us, there was Lazarus. If anyone dared to call Lazarus 'simple' in the presence of Jesus, he would stop, eyeball them, and reply, "There is nothing simple about the capacity to love. You do not know my brother, Lazarus, and, if you do not know him, you cannot know me".

And then he died. Our brother, Lazarus, became ill. We were not worried. He was robust. He got worse. We prayed. We sent word to Jesus. We had become so very scared. For our brother but also for ourselves. The vultures in our family began to circle. Everything would be lost. Lazarus lay down and could not get up. We told him Jesus was coming. That cheeky grin! Then the grimace of pain. He could not breathe. We begged him to wait for Jesus. Where was Jesus!? Lazarus died.

We buried him. We wept. We waited. Two women with no protector. Four days.

Four days!

I met Jesus some distance from our house. I had gone to meet him as soon as I heard he was near. Mary would not come. She was so angry. She screamed and she wept, and she would not come with me. I sometimes feel that I cannot say or do what I feel, that Mary takes all that space in our family and I have to be the one who hangs together. But that day.....that day I was angry too. I was shattered and furious and sad and I was hopeless. I meant to shout at him and berate him. I meant to make him feel some of the despair that I had been feeling all these days.

When I saw him, he was already weeping. People say he only wept when Mary wept, but that's not true. He ran to me, and just as I was about to open my mouth, he opened his arms and we cried into each other's hair.

"If you had been here."

"Do you believe?"

"I do."

I ran back to get Mary, told her Jesus wanted to see her. I could not keep pace with her. When I got there, she was on the ground at his feet and there were more tears. She had not been quiet. Still, she repeated, "If you had been here". Over and over. He looked broken.

At the tomb he was like a madman. "Take away the stone. Take away the stone!!"

I begged him not to shame us. Not to show his weakness to the crowd. They were not all friends. They never were. I told him there would be a smell. I told him it was too late. I said things I didn't want to say. I denied what I believed. I feared the resurrection. None of us were rational. We were stricken. We wept.

"Did I not tell you that if you believed, you would see the glory of God?", he yelled.

We took away the stone.

And Jesus looked upwards and cried, so that everyone heard him. "Father, I thank you for having heard me. I knew that you always hear me, but I have said this for the sake of the crowd standing here, so that they may believe that you sent me.'

When he had said this, he cried with a loud voice, he cried with all the rage against death that we had felt, with all the grief that burnt our hearts, with all the pain of loss, "Lazarus, come out!"

They say time stands still. It did then. There was a hush such as I have never heard before. As if all breath had stopped, in our lungs and in the whole world. Nothing happened. The mouth of the tomb gaped, a demon's maw, set to laugh in scorn.

Then, small scrabbling sounds. Shuffling. People screamed. Some fainted. Lazarus appeared, trying to walk, wrapped in grave cloths. Jesus stepped forward and took the cloth from his face. That cheeky grin. They unbound him. They let him go. He went straight to Jesus, and they held each other as the crowd slipped away. It was a holy moment. You could not watch.

Lazarus took our arms, Mary and me, and we walked home. We bathed him and dressed him.

At dinner, Jesus spoke quietly with him while we sat in awe and wonder. By morning, Lazarus was back feeding the goats with Mary. That's the oddest thing about miracles, they come and go as if nothing has happened. And yet....

Later, when we had to tell Lazarus that they had killed Jesus, he went back to his tomb and he would not come home for three days. When the news came that the disciples had seen him alive again, we ran to tell him. As we got close, we saw him laughing with someone. We knew, immediately, who it was. We left them to talk.

We believed.

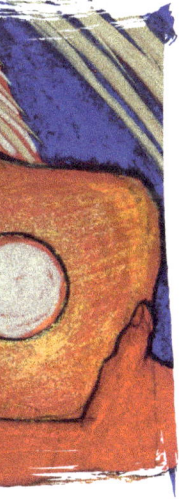

REFLECT:

What are your responses to the story? How does the story change, seeing the situation from the perspective of Martha? Are there things you have understood about the character, or the encounter, that were not in your thinking before? What is your emotional response? Are there things that make you angry? Or sad? Or happy? Or.....? Does this imaginative retelling ring true to you? Why? Why not?

QUOTE:

"If creation is good, as Genesis 1 repeatedly claims, then disability is good. This linkage is most pointed in genetic disability, which is not a result of a breakdown in the created order (a fall), but of nature's creative capacity. From single-celled organisms through to the unfathomable diversity of species that have thrived (and gone extinct) during Earth's history, the wonders of the natural world are a consequence of genetic variability, of so-called "mutations" that drive the process of evolution and its remarkable adaptivity. These same life-giving processes also generate disability. The paradox of life is that potency and vulnerability go together. Because this is so, far from being a consequence of sin, disability is a good, a symbol of potent, creative, beauty, a testimony to the generativity and limits of nature."

Professor Shane Clifton[1]

AN ABM RESPONSE:

In communities where survival is the main goal, where poverty exists as an everyday reality, the disabled are often those who suffer the most. ABM is humbled by the incredible work done by our Partners around the world, as they support and encourage local people who have a heart to respect and work with people living with disabilities as they take agency within their own communities. ABM has proudly supported projects in the Philippines and Kenya, among others. It is through the lens of the Gospel that we are able to recognise God's unique gifting in each and every person – and to recognise, own and embrace our own disabilities.

---

1 From: Crippling Christian Theology as I Power My Wheelchair Out the Door, Theology Today 2020, Vol. 77(2) 124–137
https://www.abc.net.au/religion/crippling-christian-theology-disability-faith-and-doubt/12952958
Shane is Honorary Associate of the Centre for Disability Research and Policy at the University of Sydney. His research interests explore the intersection of disability, virtue ethics, and spirituality/theology. Shane, after an accident in 2010, lives with quadriplegia and has been working with the research team for the Australian Royal Commission into Violence, Abuse, Neglect and Exploitation against People with Disability. You can find him at Shaneclifton.com

DISCUSS:

Lazarus is one of the most mysterious characters in the Gospels. If he was the 'man' of the house, why is it Mary and Martha who seem to feature most in the stories? Why does he not have any recorded interactions with Jesus, apart from being raised from the dead? And why did Jesus love him so much? Again, we often tend not to interrogate the scripture in the way we might do we other texts. In a highly patriarchal society, how do we explain the fact that the women are running the place!?

There have been many ideas put forward over the centuries and the one I have run with here is not unique. The L'Arche Community has explored this idea as they have worked with the scriptures in community with disabled adults. Central to the idea is that each person is differently gifted and that we need to view each other through the eyes of love (the Gospel lens) in order to see the gift each person brings to the world.

Painting: Loved Brothers 1, 2023

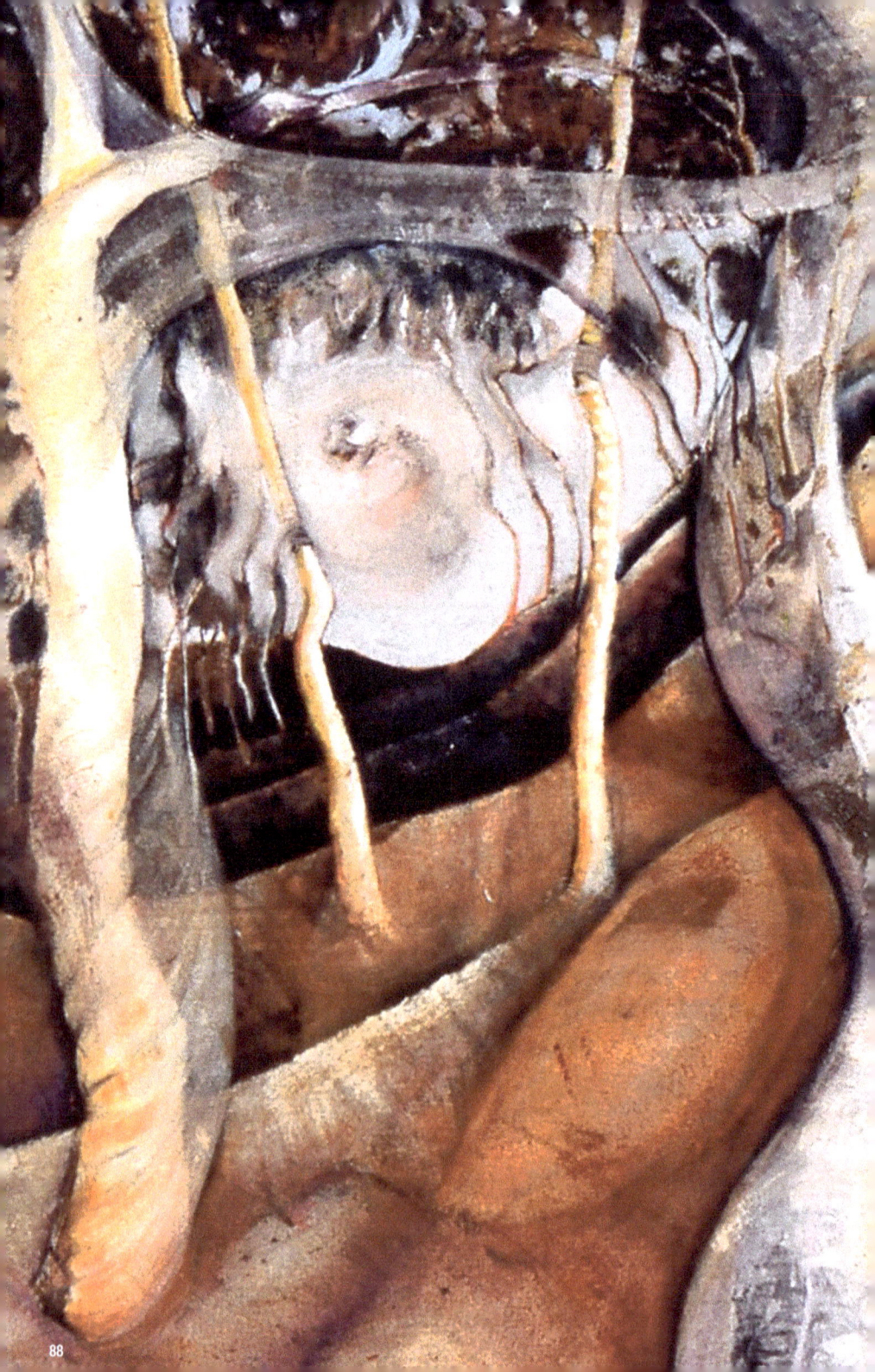

It is a dangerous fallacy to suggest that the Christian faith – following the way of Jesus – can only be done effectively by those with sufficiently rigorous, academic study of theology. Many people are often infantilised or made to feel inferior if they have not mastered the language of faith or the full scope of the scriptures. Leadership is almost never offered to those who exhibit incredible and tangible levels of faith – unless they have a degree! But the people Jesus spoke to – the people he chose as his disciples - as he travelled around were, like most of us, ordinary folk. Many were probably illiterate. Certainly, they will have been more religiously focussed, as they were part of a community for whom religious identity was crucial. Yet, they were certainly the same mix of passionate and indifferent, educated and ignorant, spiritual and profane as most communities are.

Sometimes we meet people and are amazed by what we might call, their 'simple' faith. Better words can be, 'trusting', 'deep', 'inarticulate' or 'profound'. Many of us come to this sort of faith as children and we then have to survive our theological and ecclesial education, trying to keep the core of that primal faith intact.

The work of mission is never to try and make sure everyone gets the faith 'right'. The work of mission is to view one another through the Gospel lens of love, and then live and act in ways that reveal the love of God for all people. Many people never respond to propositions about the faith, but do respond to the revealed person of Jesus, translated through the love of those who love him. Each of us, at our best, becomes a window through which others glimpse the divine. We are the body of Christ.

Painting: Memory of Shoalhaven Bush, 1989

QUESTIONS:

1. INDIVIDUAL

- Where did your faith come from? Was it learned from books or picked up from people of faith?

- Can you recollect a person in whom you saw (or see) great and deep faith? What did/do you see?

2. COMMUNITY

- At what level do you think our society respects the rights and gifting of the disabled?

- Do you feel that your community provides access and amenities to people living with disability to allow them to fully participate in society? If not, what might be our responsibility?

3. CHURCH

- What can we do in our own church communities to break down the walls of awkwardness that can get in the way of us genuinely connecting with (and including) those who are 'different' to us? Have you ever managed to do this as an individual or within a group?

- How might we learn to view people living with disability through the Gospel lens without being patronising?

NOTES:

Painting: Icon of the Presence, on door 2

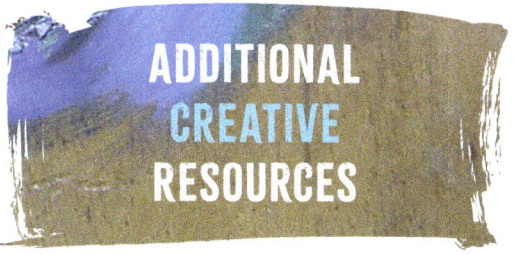

ADDITIONAL CREATIVE RESOURCES

Song:	All My Favourite People Are Broken - Over The Rhine
Google it or go to:	https://youtu.be/7Ea9uy6Mngk
	Over the Rhine is an American, Ohio-based folk music band, the core of which is the husband-and-wife team of pianist/guitarist/bassist Linford Detweiler and vocalist/guitarist Karin Bergquist.
Poetry or Prose:	**Angel** *by Terri Kirby Erickson*[2]

I used to see them walking, a middle-aged
man and his grown son, both wearing brown
trousers and white shirts like boys in a club,
or guys who like to simplify. But anyone
could see the son would never be a man who
walked without a hand to hold, a voice telling
him what to do. So the father held his son's
hand and whispered whatever it was the boy
needed to know, in tones so soft and low it
might have been the sound of wings pressing
together again and again. Maybe it was that
sound, since the father had the look of an angel
about him, or what we imagine angels should
be – a bit solemn-faced, with eyes that view
the world through a lens of kindness – who
see everyone's son as beautiful and whole.

---

2 From, 'How to Love the World', Poems of Gratitude and Hope (pg21), edited by James Crews. Storey Publishing 2021

BREAKFAST ON THE BEACH: JOHN 21:1-19

After these things Jesus showed himself again to the disciples by the Sea of Tiberias; and he showed himself in this way. Gathered there together were Simon Peter, Thomas called the Twin, Nathanael of Cana in Galilee, the sons of Zebedee, and two others of his disciples. Simon Peter said to them, 'I am going fishing.' They said to him, 'We will go with you.' They went out and got into the boat, but that night they caught nothing.

Just after daybreak, Jesus stood on the beach; but the disciples did not know that it was Jesus. Jesus said to them, 'Children, you have no fish, have you?' They answered him, 'No.' He said to them, 'Cast the net to the right side of the boat, and you will find some.' So they cast it, and now they were not able to haul it in because there were so many fish. That disciple whom Jesus loved said to Peter, 'It is the Lord!' When Simon Peter heard that it was the Lord, he put on some clothes, for he was naked, and jumped into the lake. But the other disciples came in the boat, dragging the net full of fish, for they were not far from the land, only about a hundred yards off.

When they had gone ashore, they saw a charcoal fire there, with fish on it, and bread. Jesus said to them, 'Bring some of the fish that you have just caught.' So Simon Peter went aboard and hauled the net ashore, full of large fish, a hundred and fifty-three of them; and though there were so many, the net was not torn. Jesus said to them, 'Come and have breakfast.' Now none of the disciples dared to ask him, 'Who are you?' because they knew it was the Lord. Jesus came and took the bread and gave it to them, and did the same with the fish. This was now the third time that Jesus appeared to the disciples after he was raised from the dead.

When they had finished breakfast, Jesus said to Simon Peter, 'Simon son of John, do you love me more than these?' He said to him, 'Yes, Lord; you know that I love you.' Jesus said to him, 'Feed my lambs.' A second time he said to him, 'Simon son of John, do you love me?' He said to him, 'Yes, Lord; you know that I love you.' Jesus said to him, 'Tend my sheep.' He said to him the third time, 'Simon son of John, do you love me?' Peter felt hurt because he said to him the third time, 'Do you love me?' And he said to him, 'Lord, you know everything; you know that I love you.' Jesus said to him, 'Feed my sheep. Very truly, I tell you, when you were younger, you used to fasten your own belt and to go wherever you wished. But when you grow old, you will stretch out your hands, and someone else will fasten a belt around you and take you where you do not wish to go.' (He said this to indicate the kind of death by which he would glorify God.) After this he said to him, 'Follow me.'

Painting: Peter Arrives at Breakfast, 2023

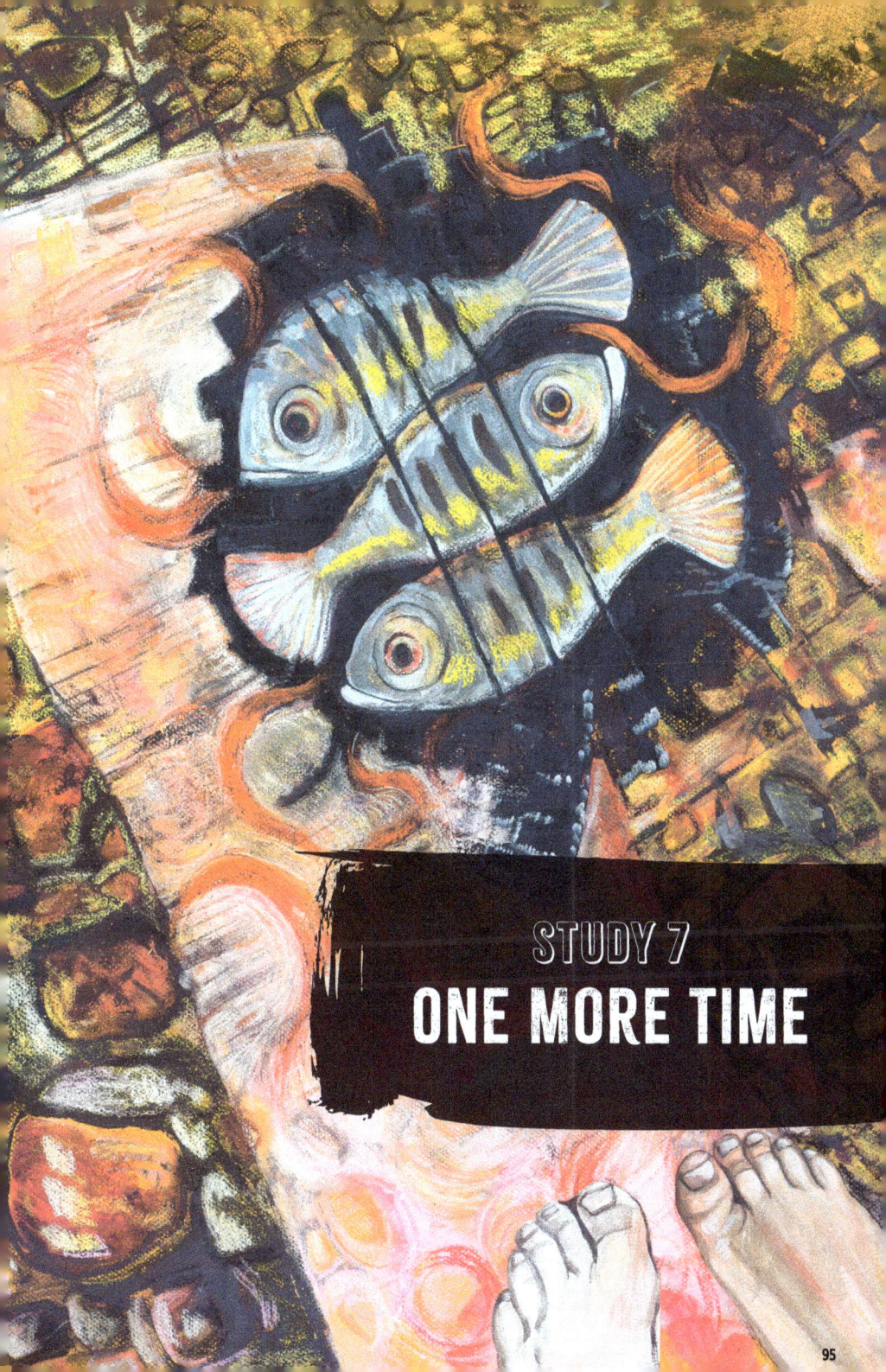

Like a dog, returning to its vomit. We went fishing.

Putting on old clothes. The water. The ropes. The sails. The nets. The stars. All so familiar. Endless stars in a clear sky. Just enough breeze to get us to a depth to put out the nets. Then silence. Seven of us and not a word between us. All night. Every hour or so we'd pull the net in, then set it again. Empty. All of us empty.

You might not understand, but you can see a miracle one day and forget it the next. It happens. You comprehend. Or you don't. You move on. We'd all seen things we never expected. We'd come to expect the unexpected. But there is still the business of being alive in the world. Still the hunger and fear and headaches and bad dreams. There is still doubt. There is still guilt.

Of course it was him, shouting from the shore. Just like the intervening years hadn't happened. Reminding us (as if we needed reminding!) that we'd walked away from any chance of an easy, simple life.

"Cast it on the right side'. Sure, why not. So, we did. And we knew, before we even took the strain. Full to bursting. All of us, full to bursting.

I needed to talk to him. But how do you talk to a man you've betrayed to his death? Who you've seen risen from the tomb? Well, you don't try it naked, that's for sure. Putting on clothes to jump into the water might seem counter-intuitive, but after the last few years, it was just another upside-down world moment. So, I swam, and the lads brought the boat in, dragging the fish.

Not that he needed fish. God only knows where he got the ones on the fire, but I wasn't going to ask him. Fish and bread. We'd been there before too. But he wanted more fish, so I ran to the boat and dragged the net onto the beach. Or rather, I helped drag that net. Big, fat fish of every kind I knew, and few that I didn't. But who asks question at a time like that.

"Come and have breakfast', he says. We sat around the fire while he cooked. Like a bunch of kids waiting for their dad to explode. Looking at our feet like we'd just discovered them. Sneaking risky glances at each other. And he just flipped the fish. And broke the bread. And fed us. Again.

People don't like to say it, but we were scared of him. Not in the way we might have once been scared of our fathers or an unjust beating. Just scared...of the mystery of him. The power. The way he could see into you. And he had a temper. Again, not about petty things, but he could let you know when you'd missed the point. As some of the stories about us report, I missed it more than most. But we loved him. Love him.

That morning on the beach, as we sat and fidgeted, he was completely there. Same as before the horror – but even more real. He'd seemed special before, but now he was something 'other', something complete and somehow more solid than the rocks and the sand and water and....us. Even so, his hands, as they tore apart the fish and passed it around, carried those scars. So broken and – now – so alive.

We had all started to relax, the words and the jokes coming a little more easily, when he called me away. 'Walk with me'.

When I was little, I had stolen a brooch of my mother's. It was the only one she had. A gift from my father, and she treasured it. I was angry about something I can't now remember. I stole it and sold it to a travelling trader. He ripped me off, of course. I had to hide the money, because where would I have got money from? I buried it. Then I couldn't remember where. My mother was distraught. She cried. For days. I helped look for the brooch, and when we couldn't find it, she cuddled me and thanked me and told me how much she loved me. I can still feel that moment, and even as I tell you my guts clench and I am so deeply, deeply ashamed.

That was nothing to what I felt as we stepped across the sand. I had a thousand things to say and no breath. He stopped, turned and looked back at the group.

'Simon son of John, do you love me more than these?'

Twist the knife. I mumbled my reply. 'Yes, Lord; you know that I love you.'

'Feed my lambs.'

The faces of the multitudes who had come to him flashed before me.

'Simon son of John, do you love me?'

'Yes, Lord; you know that I love you.' Choked out. Overwhelmed. Falling to my knees.

'Tend my sheep.'

Again, the faces of all those who had followed him, leaving home and family, faltering at the last – but not like me – not in betrayal. All wandering now.

'Simon son of John, do you love me?'

And I was on my feet and bawling, tears enough to turn the tide, because he had used the word for brotherly love. He had asked if I was still with him. 'Lord, you know everything; you know that I love you.'

'Feed my sheep. Very truly, I tell you, when you were younger, you used to fasten your own belt and to go wherever you wished. But when you grow old, you will stretch out your hands, and someone else will fasten a belt around you and take you where you do not wish to go. Follow me.'

Painting: Pastel of Hawkesbury River - Secret River, 2017

I felt the world lift and jump and glow. I looked into his eyes, and I saw myself rise from my tomb. What was broken was knit together and reinforced. He was inviting me into the 'other' I had glimpsed in him. I looked at my hands and I saw the scars forming. I looked at my friends and I saw the world bending. He placed something in my hand, and when I looked down, I was holding my mother's brooch.

"Follow me".

So I did.

REFLECT:

What are your responses to the story? How does the story change, seeing the situation from the perspective of Peter? Are there things you have understood about the character, or the encounter, that were not in your thinking before? What is your emotional response? Are there things that make you angry? Or sad? Or happy? Or.....? Does this imaginative retelling ring true to you? Why? Why not?

QUOTE:

On the whole, I do not find Christians, outside of the catacombs, sufficiently sensible of conditions. Does anyone have the foggiest idea what sort of power we so blithely invoke? Or, as I suspect, does no one believe a word of it? The churches are children playing on the floor with their chemistry sets, mixing up a batch of TNT to kill a Sunday morning. It is madness to wear ladies' straw hats and velvet hats to church; we should all be wearing crash helmets. Ushers should issue life preservers and signal flares; they should lash us to our pews.

Annie Dillard[1]

---

1   Annie Dillard, Teaching a Stone to Talk, HarperCollins, p58.

AN ABM RESPONSE:

An organisation that for over 170 years has called itself a 'mission' agency, now finds itself surrounded by groups and corporations, all with 'mission statements' and 'values flowcharts'. At one level, this is wonderful. People are taking seriously the impact they have on the world and each other, and trying to behave in ways that enhance life on earth. Certainly, some will be more sincere about this than others, but it's no bad thing to think beyond the profit margin. Every person of goodwill is an ally.

We, like Peter, are drawn on by the vision of a renewed, inclusive, compassionate world. It is in the person of Jesus, the incarnate child of God, who chose to live with us and trust us, that we find our hope. Our leader. Our reason for being. As an organisation, we carry our scars. We have made mistakes. We have had to repent. But we have also looked into the eyes of eternity, and we remain committed to the mysterious, powerful, lifechanging and ongoing work of the Gospel of Inclusion.

DISCUSS:

The Simon Peter of the Gospels is a contradictory figure. He makes great leaps of faith, then follows them up with the most astounding misunderstandings. After all this – and not withstanding his ultimate betrayal of Christ – Jesus seeks him out and restores their relationship.

I love the picture of Peter the Gospels give me. I respond to the enthusiastic love and the pig-headed ignorance. Perhaps he reminds me of myself? I love that the Gospels are willing to portray one of the great, early-church leaders as less than ideal. Much less. This is no hagiographic portrait. The picture of Peter is designed to open the door for those of us who have also loved and failed.

We live in a portion of the history of Australia – and the wider 'western' world – in which the church is struggling to find relevance. A thousand books have been written to set us straight. A thousand more have contradicted that first thousand. And here we are. Once again approaching Easter with the stubborn hope that the story matters and that the Resurrection is real.

Many scholars suggest that this passage is a later addition to the Gospel of John, designed to help people come to terms with the failure of one of the great leaders of the nascent church. Maybe it was. Maybe it wasn't. It does seem to fit beautifully with the picture of Christ we glean from the four Gospel stories. What happened on the beach that morning was as wilfully gracious and as incomprehensibly generous as the words of Jesus to the thief on the cross. Peter is welcomed back. He is fully and unreservedly included in the new world initiated in the resurrected body of Christ. Peter is given the opportunity to repent – to turn back to – and to become part of the answer. It all happens in the context of a beach BBQ and in the company of a bunch of friends. It's as prosaic as it is profound.

Church tradition suggests that between the Crucifixion and the Resurrection, Jesus 'harrowed hell'. In short, he descended to the dead and opened the gates of imprisonment so that those who chose to believe could follow him into life. Whatever we make of that strange myth, it remains true that the resurrection is the great opening of the door to life. Many of us wonder how we might encourage people to come to church and share our faith. It is possible that the answer is far simpler – and far more difficult – then we imagine.

Perhaps the work of mission is the work of opening doors for others to walk through. Perhaps it is the work of humility, through which we acknowledge our own failures and – therefore – do not expect perfection of others. Perhaps it is the allowing others to see that we truly do believe that the Resurrection is real. Perhaps it is the sharing of a meal with someone we are sure does not deserve to sit at the table with us.

Bless you and your community as you seek to follow Jesus.

QUESTIONS:

1. INDIVIDUAL

- Have you had experiences of finding deep spiritual insight in very ordinary situations?

- What has failure meant in your growth in faith? What has acceptance meant for your growth in faith?

- Are you able to sit with the experiences of shame or guilt in your life? What does that do to you, and what has been your response? What has been your experience of God's response if you have been able to face it together with God?

2. COMMUNITY

- Most politicians will do anything rather than apologise or admit failure. Why do you think this is? As a community are we incapable of supporting leaders who admit failure?

- What do you think the general community thinks about the church? Why do you think they have formed that opinion?

- What is the greatest gift the church can offer the community?

3. CHURCH

- In order to forgive or to repent, mistakes or missteps need to be acknowledged. Is that part of your church or community culture? Why? Why not?

- Peter's forgiveness and re-inclusion by Jesus seems to have been the major turning point in his life – and the life of the early church. What part has inclusivity and forgiveness played in your desire to be part of the body of Christ?

NOTES:

Painting: Icon of the Presence, 2001

ADDITIONAL CREATIVE RESOURCES

Song: Nick Cave & The Bad Seeds - Breathless

Google it or go to: https://youtu.be/1TI8xPw2aQA

Nicholas Edward Cave AO, is an Australian singer, songwriter, poet, lyricist, author, screenwriter, composer and occasional actor. He has written some of the most extraordinary songs about God, faith and spirituality.

Poetry or Prose: **The Merton Prayer** by Thomas Merton[2]

My Lord God,
I have no idea where I am going.
I do not see the road ahead of me.
I cannot know for certain where it will end.
nor do I really know myself,
and the fact that I think I am following your will
does not mean that I am actually doing so.
But I believe that the desire to please you
does in fact please you.
And I hope I have that desire in all that I am doing.
I hope that I will never do anything apart from
that desire.

And I know that if I do this you will lead me by the right road, though I may know nothing about it.

Therefore will I trust you always though
I may seem to be lost and in the shadow of death.

I will not fear, for you are ever with me,
and you will never leave me to face my perils alone.

---

2 "The Merton Prayer" from Thoughts in Solitude, 1956, 1958 by The Abbey of Our Lady of Gethsemani.

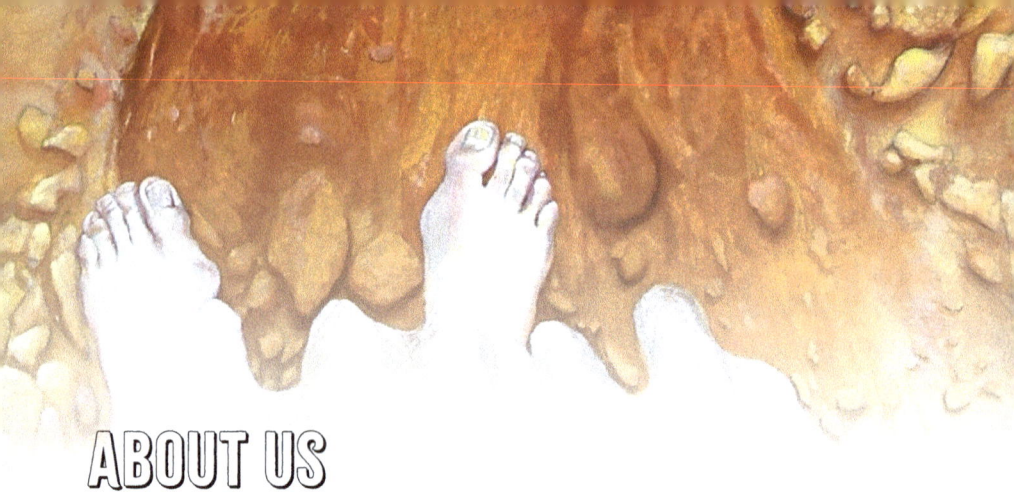

ABOUT US

ABM is the national mission agency for the Anglican Church of Australia. It is the channel through which Australian Anglicans participate in mission, both here and overseas. Through our Anglican church partners both in Australia and overseas, ABM's Church to Church program serves Aboriginal and Torres Strait Islander Anglicans as well as theological education overseas.

Anglicans in Development (AID) operates our Sustainable Communities program. AID works with church partners to deliver grassroots, community-driven development, Aboriginal and Torres Strait Islander leadership, and disaster preparedness and response.

In all our work, we want to see people everywhere experience the wholeness of life God offers in Jesus Christ, and to this end we support our partners as they participate in God's mission.

Anglican Board of Mission - Australia Ltd ABN 18 097 944 717
Local Call: 1300 302 663 | International: +61 2 9264 1021
Enquiries: info@abm.asn.au | www.abmission.org

ADDITIONAL ABM RESOURCES
Available at: www.abmission.org/resources

Songs from a Strange Land
Beautiful words and images to take you from Advent to Epiphany with a particular emphasis on Indigenous Christianity, the Australian landscape and Creation theology. Available as an app or 158-page booklet.

Into the Desert
40 days of Scripture readings, reflections and prayers for Lent that take you on a spiritual journey into the Australian wilderness. Available as an app or an 88-page booklet.

Deep calls to Deep
A 46-day journey into the mystery of suffering that begins in Holy Week and ends on Ascension Day. Available as an app or download a free 148pg pdf.

Repairing the Breach
Examines what it means to be people of healing in a broken world. Includes seven studies that take you from Ash Wednesday to Palm Sunday. Available as a 110-page booklet.

Where do we go from here?
Missional Bible Studies based on the book of Acts. Enter into the great adventure of 'mission' in our own time and place. In Australia. Today. Available as an 88-page booklet.

Climate for Change
Urges people of faith and hope to become activists for a sustainable future. Our children and grandchildren will inherit the fruit of our decisions. Available as a 64-page booklet.

A Voice in the Wilderness:
Listening to the Statement from the Heart
A study to open up conversations about the theological response to the Statement from the Heart. Available as a free pdf or 120-page booklet.

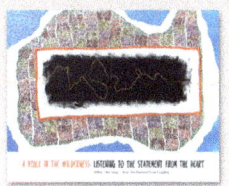

God was on Both sides of the Beach
A 5-part video study introducing the Anglican Church in the Torres Strait and the Coming of the Light, a largely unknown story but one that is important for us all to learn from.

Sustainable Development
A Bible Study guide to the Global Goals for Sustainable Development.

Free pdf, Leader's Guide or to purchase hard copies of this book:
www.abmission.org/resources/the-imaginary-doorway

ACKNOWLEDGMENTS

In any publication that comes from ABM, the most important acknowledgement is that of our Partners and the work they carry out in the communities they live in and love. ABM staff have had the opportunity to meet and befriend many people across the world. We have learnt much from our encounters with Christians living in challenging and culturally diverse environments. We have been gently guided towards a fuller understanding of what God is doing in the world and have been generously invited to participate. So, to all our Partners, past, present and future – thank you!

I also wish to acknowledge my ABM colleagues, people touched by a desire to help make the world a better place through love, hope and justice. It's an improbable outcome and an often-frustrating challenge, but they just get on with it. The 'now, but not yet' kingdom of God is built by people who dare to try, dare to dream, dare to act. You are admirable people.

One of the other things we learn as we travel, is that people's culture, language and context can differ vastly, but that humans are often motivated by very similar things. Family, community, love, hope, respect, kindness – and faith. The story of faith, the story of Jesus, has transposed itself into virtually every country and continent. Somehow, the very real and grounded story of a young Jewish rabbi who we believe to be the Son of God, reaches into the lives, hearts and minds of people wherever it is told. That is the power of story.

The Gospel is a story. It began as a rumour shared between frightened but hopeful disciples and grew into an unstoppable wave of life-giving affirmation of all that God has made. It has been written down. But that's not the Gospel. It has been twisted and corrupted by some. But that's not the Gospel. It has been hijacked by principalities and powers. But that's not the Gospel. The Gospel is the story that, through the working of the Holy Spirit, has whispered words of liberation and love, rebellion and release, courage and compassion, into the hearts of billions. Stories change the world.

Vanessa and I have been telling and re-telling the Gospel story for most of our lives. We acknowledge all those who have taught us and told us stories, nurturing our doubt and our faith. Communities, parishes and friends. And we give thanks for our families – especially our children, who remind us that telling the story in never enough. It has to be lived.

Steve Daughtry, Epiphany 2023